ON BEING GOD

ON BEING GOD

indestructible joy

DOUGLAS HARDING

The Shollond Trust
London

Published by The Shollond Trust
87B Cazenove Road, London N16 6BB, England
www.headless.org
headexchange@gn.apc.org

The Shollond Trust is a UK charitable trust, reg. no. 1059551

Copyright © The Shollond Trust 2023

All rights reserved. No portion of this book may be reproduced in any form or by any means without written permission of the publisher.

ISBN 978-1-914316-45-6
Cover design: rangsgraphics.com
Interior design: Richard Lang

Preface

When Douglas Harding wrote *The Face Game* in 1968 he adapted the contents of *On Being God*, an unpublished work of about fifty short chapters he had written several years before. Harding did a superb job of morphing *On Being God* into *The Face Game*, a book that took Transactional Analysis to a new level, beyond psychology into Enlightenment. But happily, the original chapters of *On Being God* were still in Harding's papers after he died, for they have a tone and message that is different from the form they took in *The Face Game*. *On Being God* stands on its own as a powerful, inspiring text.

There are several influences, several spiritual traditions, detectable in *On Being God*.

Harding's greatest though not his best-known book, *The Hierarchy of Heaven and Earth*, was published in 1952. Everything that Harding later wrote in one way or another drew inspiration from that opus magnum. As he used to say, "It's all in *The Hierarchy*". However, in the late 1950s, some six years after finishing *The Hierarchy*, Harding discovered Zen through the writings of D.T. Suzuki and others. Harding's best-known book *On Having No Head* connected *headlessness* with Zen and was published by the Buddhist Society in 1961. Just after *On Having No Head* Harding wrote *Zen Experience*, again connecting *headlessness* with Zen. The style of both these books is different from the more complex and philosophical *Hierarchy*. They are infused with the down-to-earth directness and simplicity of Zen, the discovery and expression of our 'true nature' in ordinary life. It was during this same period that Harding also wrote *On Being God*. However, this book is different. In it Harding mentions Zen only once. Instead the imagery and language, as the title indicates, is Christian, the faith of Harding's childhood. After being out East (virtually, through reading Suzuki) Harding had returned to the West, as it were, and had shared his understanding of and enthusiasm for Zen—in *On Having No Head* and *Zen Experience*. But now, in *On Being God*, Harding put Zen aside and went back to his Christian roots. Even so, the essence of Zen pervades every page—its fearlessness, its brevity, its everydayness, even its humour. In the true spirit of Zen, Harding retained the spirit of Zen whilst dropping the form.

Harding was both deeply knowledgeable of and proud of his Christian heritage. He was so familiar with the lives and writings of the great mediaeval European mystics, it was as if he knew them personally. Though in *On Being God* Harding doesn't mention them by name, they are there in the background. Harding's bold declaration that he is not seeing God *as Harding* but *as God Himself* is reminiscent of Meister Eckhart's "the eye through which I see God is the same eye through which God sees me", or Saint Catherine of Genoa's "My Me is God, nor do I recognise any other Me but my God Himself". These great mystics bravely proclaimed the reality of their divinity, thereby risking the charge of blasphemy. Harding felt close to them. But more than that, he saw he was *one* with them, consciously living from the same indivisible, infinitely creative Source. Of course, Harding was in no danger of being burned at the stake for saying he was God. Nevertheless he knew that he would upset the traditionalists. Though that didn't matter to Harding. He relished being a rebel. *On Being God* has a mischievous, irreverent spirit running through it. (There again it is Zen-like.) Harding was aware he was barefacedly, *no-facedly*, challenging those around him who were attached to the form of their religion.

Alongside Zen and Christianity is a third spiritual tradition present in the background of this book, another community of truth-sayers in whose company Harding felt at home. The *Upanishads*, the great scriptures of north India, were composed some three thousand years ago. Singing of the Alone—*as* the Alone—they use the language of the *First Person*. The *Avadhut Gita* declares: "I alone am, ever free from all taint. The world exists like a mirage within me. To whom shall I bow?" And the *Kaivalya Upanishad* proclaims: "I am in all, all are in Me." In *On Being God* Harding, singing also *as* the Alone, also uses the language of the *First Person*—language in which from time to time he becomes ecstatic: "I laugh and shout My head off. This is what it is to be God Almighty—this roar of delight, this gasping incredulity, this trembling awe, this fathomless ignorance which is the highest knowledge. My God, how *did* I do It?" Harding is aware that his joy—astonishing fact!—does not belong to *himself-as-Harding* but to *Himself-as-God*. His joy is *God's very own joy at His own Being,* the "indestructible joy" of having happened. You as God have carried off the 'impossible but true' feat of pulling yourself by your own bootstraps out of the deepest darkest night of non-being. The greatest magic trick ever! *On Being God* is a *gita*, a song of adoration and praise *to* the One, *by* the One—a modern *Upanishad*.

However, more important than the religious traditions that Harding was inspired by was a principle Harding relied on whenever he responded to the question 'What am I?' (It is the principle at the heart of *The Hierarchy of Heaven and Earth*): *I am the sole and final authority on what it is like to be me. Only I am where I am, so only I am in a position to say what it is like here.* Harding described each of the chapters in *On Being God* as "an exercise in radical self-examination". In the early 1970s Harding developed his *experiments*—awareness exercises that guide attention to one's central identity. They are called *experiments* because *they test a hypothesis*—Harding was as much a scientist as a mystic—the hypothesis that *what you are for yourself at no distance is the absolute opposite of what you are for others, from whatever distance they are observing you.* Harding's experiments are immensely important because they make available, *at will*, the *experience* of our central reality. They catapult us from just thinking or talking about the Self, vaguely and inconclusively, to clearly and indubitably *seeing* the Self. Therefore they enable anyone so inclined to live consciously *as* the Self. Opening the way to "the God-seeing life", as the great mediaeval Ruysbroeck (a favourite of Harding's) described it, they make it possible to *live your life aware that you are God living your life!* Now there's an invitation to an adventure for you! These chapters are the forerunners of those experiments. Each is a modern pointer, a meditation—a *two-way* meditation—inviting you to look—to look *to see if you are God.*

There will never be a better moment than now for enjoying the Beatific Vision, the realisation that you are the self-originating One-that-Alone-Is!—the headless God that is, in this very moment now, reading these words.

Richard Lang

Contents

Preface	v
Prologue	1
1 Headlessness	5
2 Boundlessness	7
3 Immortality	9
4 The Mirror	11
5 The Two Species	13
6 Clear-headedness	15
7 Detachment	17
8 Astonishment	19
9 Sight	21
10 Meaning	23
11 Perfection	25
12 God	27
13 The Ordinary	29
14 No Brain	31
15 No Body	33
16 The Inanimate	35
17 Foolishness	37
18 Indifference	39
19 Asymmetry	41
20 Idleness	43
21 Heaven	45
22 The Universe	49
23 Advertisements	51
24 Subjectivity	53
25 The Face	55

26	Hands	57
27	Love	59
28	The Seen	61
29	Centrality	63
30	Education	65
31	Novelty	67
32	Allness	69
33	Creation	71
34	Satisfaction	73
35	Emptiness	75
36	Opinions	77
37	Presence	79
38	Home	81
39	Freedom	83
40	Aloneness	85
41	Paradox	87
42	Self-Concern	89
43	Omniscience	91
44	Omnipotence	93
45	Omnipresence	95
46	Discrimination	99
47	Enlightenment	101
48	Deification	103
49	Spiritual Exercises	105
50	Stopping Thought	109
51	Self-Confidence	113
	Epilogue	117

Note to the Reader

This book demands the whole of the reader's courage and sincerity. It insists that he shall start all over again, dropping all ideas about what he's supposed to be, and taking a fresh look at himself to see what he actually is. If he will only dare to do this he is promised an astounding discovery and an immense reward. The discovery isn't merely that he's not what he thought he was, but its opposite in all respects. And the reward isn't merely happiness, but indestructible joy.

Each of the fifty-one short chapters is an exercise in radical self-examination, leading to nothing less than Deification.

Prologue

Who Am I?

In the name of religion, immense claims are made for man — claims which are, to say the least, ill-founded. Take the inescapable fact of death. Why should man — including day-old infants and the lowest imbeciles — be immortal, while the higher apes and pigs and fleas and flowers are mortal? Or take the question of free will. Is it anything more than wishful thinking to suppose that man, alone amongst creatures, can ever break loose from his inherited constitution and environment, and so become capable of a truly independent, spontaneous deed?

All such claims made on man's behalf boil down to the claim that he is not what he seems — a mere man — but what he doesn't seem — a superman or god. The doctrine is that somehow he is like God, or contains God, or is a son of God, or is even God Himself travelling incognito. The disguise is certainly thorough. One doesn't have to go to the trouble of comparing his embryo or his skeleton or his brain with those of an ape or a frog, to see that this pretence of deification will not do. To glance at him is enough. Does a man look like the Creator of the universe? Does he behave as He might be supposed to behave, or feel as He might feel? Is he big enough, powerful enough, permanent enough, knowledgeable enough, wise enough, free enough, independent enough, calm enough, to pose as even a minor god or godling without raising a laugh?

No: let us face it — man is man. He is just what he evidently is — small, local, mortal, conditioned, weak, agitated, unstable:

in short, precisely the opposite of any God deserving that title. Really it is astonishing that any confusion could ever have arisen between them. What but escapism, make-believe on the grandest scale, could account for such blindness to obvious facts?

Because this divine-human confusion has infected so much of our religious experience and thinking from the earliest times till today, a clean break must be made. It is necessary to start again, with a disinfected and open mind, determined not to rely upon any tradition, scripture, teacher, or pre-conceived opinion, but instead to face the facts just as they are given, no matter how strange they may look. When *all* voices are silent, the facts speak for themselves.

What is true Enlightenment but just this facing the facts, in all honesty and simplicity? It is going by what one clearly sees for oneself, and no longer by what one is told or imagines. It is having the courage to fit the world to one's perceptions, instead of one's perceptions to the world. It takes with *complete* seriousness whatever is presented, without judging it or improving upon it in any way.

This is quite different from that other, perhaps more familiar definition of Enlightenment, as the *complete* realisation that (contrary to all appearances) one is nothing less than Buddha, or Brahman, or Absolute Mind, or the Whole, or God Himself—the One Reality, Who is alone and without a second.

On the face of it, these two definitions of Enlightenment flatly contradict each other. It seems I must choose either the first (which tells me to be honest) or the second (which tells me to be God), and that to combine them is impossible. For if I were to take both as valid at once, this could only mean that when I look honestly at myself I see God—which is surely absurd.

But is it necessarily absurd? After all, it is conceivable that my manhood and not my divinity is an illusion. In that case I should be able to see plainly Who I am: I should look like God and not at all like a man; for God and man are poles apart, and He is unlikely to look like anyone but Himself. Also it is improbable that He peers at Himself through a fog, or detects His own nature with difficulty: and if I am none other than He, then unbiassed inspection should immediately reveal the fact, with ease and unclouded brilliance; and it should go on to disclose that I am in every respect the opposite of human.

What, in fact, does my self-inspection reveal—God or man? When I reject all hearsay and dare to look for myself, as if for the first time, what do I find? God and man are so incompatible, so utterly different, that I cannot be both. Which, then, am I?

In each section of the enquiry that follows, I have examined an aspect of myself, comparing what I see myself to be with what I see others to be. In order to help to distinguish as clearly as possible between 'the two Species', between God on the one hand and man on the other, the pronouns belonging to God have capitals—He, Him, Me, Mine, Myself, and so on—and in no instance do they belong to any man. Least of all do they belong to the one called Douglas Harding, whose birth certificate I hold, whom I observe daily in the mirror to be all too human, and who will soon be a mess of decaying matter. Of all the men I know fairly well, he is perhaps the least worthy of divine honours, and the most anxious to disclaim them.

* * * * *

Chapter 1

Headlessness

A Man Has A Head: I Have No Head

Forgetting myself, I start the adventure of self-discovery all over again, but as if for the first time. Quick, before the screen of memory blots out sight! What does my face look like now, this very instant? How many eyes, mouths, noses, ears have I? What shape and colour are they? Where are they? Without thinking now: how big is this head—bigger than a pea, smaller than the sky?

Examination of this spot with a fresh and open mind reveals not the slightest trace of eyes, mouth, ears, hair, skin, bone, blood, brain. Try as I may, I can find here no outline, no cloud, no tint, however faint. In fact, there never was anything here: I only imagined it.

It won't do to say that my head is really here, though hidden from me. Only I am well placed to observe what's here, and if it's hidden from me it is truly absent. The situation is not that I can't see what's here, but that only I can, and that I see Nothing. As if anyone *there* could talk me out of what I find *here*, or is in any position to try!

Nor will it do to say that I can feel my head with my fingertips. I can't. I see that what I am fingering is a phantom so empty and transparent and colourless that it could scarcely be less like a head. A man could have a glass eye, but scarcely a glass head, and remain human!

Nor do the other senses help: in fact, they disclose everything but the missing head. Just as I see outer objects and not eyes, so I hear sounds, not ears; taste food, not a tongue; smell odours, not a nose; feel heat and cold and pain, not nerve endings. If I go by my senses here and now, I have only one 'sense organ'—this remarkable Void, this 'hole where a head should have been'.

As for my head in my shaving mirror, it's not at all what I'm looking for. It's in the wrong place, cut off, too small, round the wrong way, without sides or back, and intangible. In short, it's a phantom out there, which may look like a head but *feels* like nothing, and the exact opposite of this other phantom here, which may feel like a head but *looks* like nothing. And I can find no way of bringing the two phantoms together here and making something of them.

This is the riddle: who is it that needs no head to see the world? Who is this brainless one who is nevertheless now putting this question about himself?

Obviously he is not Douglas Harding or any other man, or any earthly creature. Could he be anything less than divine?

* * * * *

Chapter 2

Boundlessness

A Man Is Small: I Am Boundless

What I find in place of a head is neither a point, nor a head-shaped and head-sized cavity, nor a huge empty hole without edges, but all of space filled with the world's profusion. If I am anything at all, I am everything, for quite evidently I have no boundaries whatever. If I own or contain that severed head over there in the camera or the picture frame, or in that second bathroom behind the shaving mirror, if I own or contain these four largish limbs radiating from this decapitated trunk, then along with them I own or contain all the smaller heads and trunks and limbs (animal as well as human) that come and go in this great space of mine. The many-headed, many-limbed gods of the East may not be very good likenesses of Me, but they give the idea.

I trust the data, and go by what things look like. I have only to glance around to *see* that a man is small and that I am huge, and that he is never more than a piece of Me. And this agrees perfectly with what I *feel* about him—he is of varying but never overriding importance: one of many, he must take his chance with them. And, even more certainly, it agrees with what I feel about Myself—I am unique, supremely important, without any rival whatsoever. It would be mock modesty—worse, it would be quite dishonest—to pretend that I have ever put Myself on a level with anyone else. Decades of intense indoctrination, almost every minute of every hour from the nursery down to the present moment, haven't begun to persuade Me that I am only a part of the Whole. I know otherwise. In My heart I have always been sure that I am infinite, absolute, all-inclusive, the world conqueror. Someone asks: who do I think I am? There is only one answer that rings true and is satisfying and quite final: I am He. I am immense; I am All.

They were right, of course, about Douglas Harding. And, now at last I see that little man where he is and always has been — over there and never, never for one moment, here — I can afford to think no more highly of him than of any other mortal. It is incredible how I refused for so many years to trust the plain evidence, and foisted him upon this Place, mixing the human with the divine. No wonder I was always thinking far, far too much of him, and far, far too little of Myself.

And the welcome paradox is that, now I see My Vastness here as wholly distinct from his smallness there, it wholly embraces it and 'saves' it.

* * * * *

Chapter 3

Immortality

A Man Is Born And Dies:
I Am Unborn And Undying

Was I ever born? Certainly I have no experience of starting to experience, of beginning to be; and how can I honestly or meaningfully speak of any time from which I am altogether absent? Again, what ancestry could I have?

Parents resemble their offspring, and what human or animal parent has ever resembled this headless Oddity? What other specimens of this strange Species have occurred? What doctor would write a live birth certificate for that unheard-of monster — a headless baby? From what still vaster Mother could be born this already boundless space which is itself the matrix of all creatures?

Shall I ever die? How could I experience the end of all experience, or be conscious of final unconsciousness? Besides, it is surely the born who die, and I own to no birthday. What is the death rate in My Species, and what precedent is there for My dying? What doctor would write out a death certificate for a patient who had always been decapitated? Of course, those four limbs out there are already disintegrating, and that familiar head on the other side of the mirror goes on ageing and will presently disappear never to return, but there is nothing *here* to decay or suffer the least change. This no-head will never go grey or wrinkled, or get a second older than it has ever been. No disaster can touch this Container of all disasters.

I am told that everything perishes — every plant, animal, man, race, species, planet, star, galaxy. And My own observation of the world confirms this verdict: I see mortality all around. But I see it from the station of immortality. Here is the Universal Registrar of Births and Deaths (from this Galaxy's down to Douglas Harding's and beyond), the changeless background against which all change becomes evident. But if I am above all decay and alteration, that is because I am also below them. Indeed it's not that I am too exalted to die, but rather that I die every moment the deepest of all deaths, the death right down into the bottomless abyss of nonentity, of indescribable Nothingness, so that even the most moribund of creatures is, beside Me (or better, in Me), as alive as can be. The least flicker of any life of My own would be enough to kill all who live in Me, and I should no longer be Full of life.

These aren't pious phrases of comfort and hope; still less are they interesting speculation. Nothing could be more vivid, more immediate, or more practical and handy, than this clear vision of immortality here and now. I see — I see that I am — at this moment, that pure and brilliant Void which is more obviously free from birth and death than the man it replaces is trapped in them.

* * * * *

Chapter 4

The Mirror

A Man Sees Himself In The Mirror: I See Someone Else

He says he is there in the mirror. Apparently it isn't somebody else who is shaving himself in that bathroom behind the glass, but the same man as the one who is shaving himself in this bathroom in front of the glass. And he's quite right. One can see exactly what he means: there are indeed two closely similar men, one on this side of the glass and one on that, staring fixedly at each other while they shave. He is duplicated, in two places at once, and finds nothing strange or frightening in this. It is the human condition to be plural and beside oneself, and quite happy not to know *where* one is.

I notice that I, too, am confronted by a man whenever I stand before the mirror, and it is always the same man—all the time changing and growing older, but still recognisably himself. And I, too, find this familiar face fascinating—but for the opposite reason: not because it is so like but because it is so unlike Mine. Obviously he needs to shave that stubbly chin, while I wait idly here observing how clean My Face is, not only of beard, but of chin and cheeks and every other feature. In fact, this room is unoccupied.

As I watch that white-haired, middle-aged, staring man, unblinking and left-handed, busy shaving in *that* room, it is as if a great flood sweeps through *this* room, carrying away everything human, everything alive, everything existent. In this wonderful Bathroom I bathe indeed: here, I am washed clean of body, mind, life, motion, and all change, clean of all that involved mass of human and animal and material contamination which confronts Me there in the next room. And what is still more wonderful is how intensely this Cleanliness here is alive to Itself as spotless through and through, without ever having to go an inch outside Itself to see Itself. I am only *here*. And because I know where I am I know what I am. This truly is Home Ground and Holy Ground, the Gate of Heaven and the pure Temple of God.

The mirror, then, has a divine as well as a human use: it never lies, but plainly shows where man is and where God is, and what man is and what God is. My glass brings out with the utmost vividness the total distinction between Douglas Harding and Myself, leaving no excuse for confusion.

Man abhors the obvious. It doesn't take a subtle or spiritual or highly trained mind to see the mirror's revelation: quite the contrary, it is such a mind which blocks the seeing. All that is needed is the childlike—almost the idiotic—simplicity to see what there actually is to see, without thinking about it, and to trust it utterly.

* * * * *

Chapter 5

The Two Species

My friend agrees (indeed, he insists) that he is a man, just as I have described him—headed, mortal, finite, and so on: and, after all, he should know. Besides, when he tells Me he has a head, I notice that it is the head itself speaking, thus removing the last doubt. And when I point out that I have no head, I notice that it is this no-head, this Void, which says so: again, what could be more convincing? What further proofs are needed of our total incompatibility? Truly we are quite alien Species.

It might be objected that, in fact, there are not two *Species*, but one Species having two *aspects*—call them body and spirit, or finite and infinite, or human and divine, as preferred. Every man (the objection continues) is thus two-sided; but I take all the better side and naturally appear superhuman or even divine, while the others are left with all the worse side and naturally appear all too human or even subhuman.

My answer is that I see two places a few feet apart, called Here and There, and the first is God's and the second man's. Imagine our two Species on show at some enterprising Zoo, in quite separate but adjacent cages—Mine labelled *Deus*, his labelled *Homo sapiens*, var. *Harding* (male), and the dividing bars set so that neither specimen can invade the other's enclosure. Of course our keeper is entitled to say that we are really two aspects of a single specimen, but this remark in no way weakens the iron bars that keep us for ever apart, or does anything to lessen the absolute contrast between what is on one side and what is on the other.

But my real answer is that I did not set out to theorise or moralise but to *look*, with an open mind, and to take seriously whatever I saw, no matter what the consequences. My aim was at all costs to take what I found without explaining it away; and if My findings have turned out to be about as shocking and revolutionary as they could be, that was perhaps to be expected. And though they are indeed strange, they aren't therefore absurd: on the contrary, this 'two-Species philosophy' is the only one I know which works out in practice and in theory. I can make little sense, and less use, of the others.

And if My findings have also turned out to be unimaginably happy, can I complain? Should I dismiss them as too good to be true, and start looking here for something less gloriously exalting? No: the infinite rewards of honest Self-investigation have to be accepted fearlessly, in the same straightforward spirit—the spirit of true enquiry which trusts the given, even when *All* is given.

* * * * *

Chapter 6

Clear-headedness

He Is Muddle-headed: I Am Clear-headed

One frame of reference — the common-sense or humanist — and nothing fits; *two* frames — the human and the divine, *that* place and *this* place — and every piece glides into position. A false and premature unity makes real Oneness impossible. Discrimination must come first.

To be man is to have many pressing problems: to be God is to have none. The problems are man's, not Mine; and the strange thing is that when I see them in this light they are instantly solved, and solved most thoroughly in the only possible way. When I enjoy in *this* Frame the spotless canvas, in *that* a riot of colour, then canvas and paint come together in the perfect picture. Because there is no confusion between the Emptiness here and its Fullness there, between the divine Ground and its human superstructure, between this Centre and those regions yonder, there remains no contradiction between them and no outstanding problems anywhere.

In other words, I am the Solution of all human problems, but not on their own level. I resolve them by being Myself here where no problem arises, and perfectly detached from the world over there where no problem is cleared up.

This is no pious platitude, but the precise and practical answer to the great questions that have plagued and baffled mankind for millenniums; it is the rationale that works. To take an example: does free will exist? This well-worn puzzle is totally insoluble within the one, common-sense frame of reference, and totally solved within the two frames. Freedom is here, bondage there—it's as simple as that. It isn't a case of *one* being who is partly bound and partly free, but *two*—the first is the man there who is wholly bound because he is plainly a mere part of the world-system, while the second is the God here Who is wholly free because He is plainly no part of any system, but contains all systems. There is no third position, intermediate between human bondage and divine freedom.

As will perhaps become clearer in the course of this enquiry, it is the same with the other major problems that trouble philosophers and theologians—the problems of knowledge, time, space, causation, creation, good and evil, life and death, and so on—they are cleared up once they are seen as not Mine. They aren't at all discounted or airily dismissed, but *placed*; they are seen for what they are where they are, and so give no more trouble. This is what it is to be really clear-headed.

* * * * *

Chapter 7

Detachment

He Is Attached: I Am Detached

I can *see* that a man is attached to the world — to his limbs, clothes, furniture, house, car, family, city, and so on; I do not see him apart from these things and on his own. Wherever I meet him he is visibly continuous with his surroundings: no magic circle or no-man's-land cordons him off; no aureole keeps the profane world at a distance. All his surfaces are strongly adhesive. He is built in, one piece with the universe. Or rather, it flows through him at different rates, and there is no part of him which is not part of the flux.

And what I see, he confirms. He freely admits that he is not himself when parted from even a few of these appendages: he suffers when they deteriorate, is glad when they improve, and relies on them always. For they make something of him, extend his physique as truly as any flesh-and-blood limb does; they body him forth. Nor need he feel ashamed of holding on for dear life to the apparatus he must have to express himself, for without it there would be no life and nothing to express.

Just as clearly as I see his attachment, I see My detachment. I actually am quite loose and broken away from all these surrounding objects. Not only can I find here no solid, no surface or line or point, to which things might stick, but I notice that anything rash enough to approach this empty Centre is exploded and emptied and utterly destroyed. I don't put My hat on My head, but lose both. My food is abolished, not digested. I am indeed no common hole, but an edgeless and sideless and bottomless mine-shaft into which all comers fall to destruction. The river of the world doesn't flow through Me: it loses itself in this immense Gulf, and arises from this same Gulf a new river.

And I find that when I *see* Myself as thus detached from the world, I *am* detached. I notice that I cannot steadily observe this central Gap or Discontinuity without observing also that I am It and perfectly independent. As consciously Nothing here, I truly am free from everything there. It isn't a matter of achieving this state, but of deeply accepting it as a fact: for Me, seeing is believing plus knowing plus feeling: or rather, it is undifferentiated Realisation, wherein theory and practice are indistinguishable.

In short, detachment comes as naturally to Me as attachment to man. The world runs like water off My back, while he is soaked to the bone.

* * * * *

Chapter 8

Astonishment

I Am Wonderful: Man Is Nothing Special

Man may sometimes find himself mildly surprising, but certainly not incredible. He is in little danger of screaming with fright, of being suddenly unmanned by the astounding spectacle of man. I, on the other hand, never begin to get used to Myself: I am dumbfounded, revelling in and adoring My absolute mysteriousness. I am the very last one to take Myself for granted.

There is nothing wrong with this immense discrepancy between the human and the divine: like all the others, it is perfectly in order. What, indeed, *is* particularly astonishing about that brief and tiny fragment called Douglas Harding? The conditioned necessarily lacks surprise: you can see it coming, you can account for it, and you can even show why it has to be what it is. Man is a cog in the universe-machine, about which more and more is known, and less and leas remains mysterious; and if that cog were lost it could be reconstructed by examining the adjacent cogs.

Unlike Me, man is nothing special, and neither wonderful nor wonderstruck. It is his very nature to be ordinary, and Mine to be extraordinary. How could I, who clearly see Myself to be the unconditioned Origin and Sum of all conditioned things, Self-originating, Self-sustaining, Alone, fail to find Myself absolutely astounding? There is only one Miracle, and I am it. The real Wonder is right here, and even the most spectacular and mysterious goings-on out there are only its casual by-products.

There is no joy like the divine Astonishment, which reduces all existences, not so much to one great Question Mark as to one great Exclamation Mark. I — yes, this very I — am the only one that is: Douglas Harding and all the others are merely My fantasy, My dream-toys. I have no friend to share My astonishment or to congratulate Me, no audience to applaud: these words are a soliloquy, My private pleasure. There is only Myself, without a dust-grain to bear Me company. What an incomparable achievement, what success, what audacity, what splendour! The fact that I go on effortlessly to throw off innumerable worlds teeming with gods and men and unspeakable riches of every kind — this is nothing at all, given Myself.

And what a Joke it is! I laugh and shout My head off. *This* is what it is to be God Almighty — this roar of delight, this gasping incredulity, this trembling awe, this fathomless ignorance which is the highest knowledge.

My God, how *did* I do It?

* * * * *

Chapter 9

Sight

Man Has Eyes And Is Blind:
I Have No Eyes And See

I see, not because I have eyes, nerves, brain, but because I haven't: they would merely block the view. Only this perfectly clear head, emptied of itself and exploded to infinity, could be void enough and big enough to contain the universe. This is no theory: I see it to be so, here and now. These eyes are so wide-open they have merged into one Eye, and that one Eye has vanished, along with all that lies around and behind it.

A man has quite a different story to tell. It seems he must have the very thing I must not have—a head—before he can see. For looking at the universe *he* requires a spherical observatory, about the size of a small sputnik and similarly packed with delicate apparatus. Are there, then, two antithetical ways of seeing the same world—the divine which sees without eyes, and the human which sees with them?

It seems improbable. Moreover, the second story—the human—makes no sense. How could a few cubic inches of brain tissue secrete, or find room for, or somehow collect and condense, the universe, and what sign do they give of performing any such miracle? The truth is that, no matter how elaborate their sensory equipment, heads no more *see* the world than sputniks or cameras or electronic eyes do: they are only in communication with it—which is a very different thing.

Man is a very small part of the universe, and though he

is in all directions bound to (and indeed continuous with) the remainder, it is still outside him. Thanks to extremely effective signalling and other means of communication, he is always influencing and being influenced by distant objects, but they stay distant, and they stay themselves, and he stays himself. They are not present to him, not presented to him. He doesn't *see* them. I go by what I see: and *I have never seen a man see*. It's true I see his face light up in response (say) to a proffered £5 note, but I observe that the face and the note don't merge, or change places, or abolish one another. How different from Me! My Face doesn't light up, doesn't respond to the bank-note: it *is* the bank-note!

If the seen doesn't totally wipe out the seer there is no seeing, but only signalling. I notice that all over the world this signalling is going on, but only *here* is there seeing. I am the only Seer, and I see that I am Nothing. The God here who has no eyes, sees the man there who has eyes and is blind.

* * * * *

Chapter 10

Meaning

His World Is Meaningful: Mine Is Meaningless

The proper work of man is to build himself a universe out of chaos, to take the sticks and straws of raw Nature and weave a shelter for himself, a place he is comfortable in and knows his way around, a home that means the world to him, so that without it he isn't himself at all.

Accordingly he names all things, classifies them, compares and contrasts them, links them with one another and himself in countless ways, till each object is a little knot in a vast net, held firmly in place and lacking all distinction. Only connect! Everything has its deep significance, its spiritual or poetic overtones, its vocabulary, its world-wide associations, its uses, its heavy burden borne in from the past and carried out into the future. Nothing is just itself, but is made by and makes what is not itself. It is a finger pointing to other fingers which are pointing to... and so on. Man's world is always Monday, when everybody is taking in everybody else's washing, and everybody is looking rather drab because all his nice things are at the laundry.

My world is Tuesday, when the washing comes back and everybody is wearing his own best and gayest clothes, all spotlessly clean and colourful—and perfectly meaningless. Their value is intrinsic; they are themselves, and nothing to do with each other, and—above all—nothing to do with Me. Now shapes come into their very own shapeliness, colours glow with an intense inner fire, music is twice as thrillingly melodious, scents outscent themselves, tastes have a new tang and savour—all because they have broken loose from man's world (the world that patiently ties itself up in knots), and dropped their heavy load of meaning and are on holiday. And it is part of the holiday spirit that I see no reason in them or behind them, no necessity for them either to be or to be what in fact they so delightfully are, no lurking symbolism, no practical axes for them to grind, no uplifting spiritual lessons for them to teach, no moral for them to point, no principle for them to illustrate, no law for them to obey. On Tuesday I see only what I see. And the view, unlike Monday's dull landscape, is perfectly enchanting. In all seriousness I declare that *nothing* here is ugly, or tiresome, or commonplace, or out of place. Every chance patterning of living leaves on a stem, of dead leaves on a path, of clouds, of tree bark and wood grain, of pebbles on the beach, of stains on old walls, of the food on one's plate, of litter and junk—every single one is a perfect arrangement, quite lovely. Even human artefacts are all beautiful on Tuesday.

But Tuesday's world doesn't abolish Monday's. I neither deprive the human world of one iota of its rich internal significance nor add one iota of My own. I have no meaning whatever to make it a present of. It, too, is *all right!*

* * * * *

Chapter 11

Perfection

His World Is Unsatisfactory: Mine Is Perfect

My mind and body are evacuated with a total voiding, container along with contents. For to be or to have anything is to forfeit consciousness: there is no consciousness in the world except in the place called Here, where nobody exists. Holding on to nothing whatever—least of all to Myself—I am truly aware of Myself as Myself and here and perfect.

And of My world as perfect too. The only way to clean up the world is to come clean, and cease spoiling it by withholding those very things which would put it right. I see it all as perfect because I *face* it all and keep none of it back; I see it as sane because it is all *there*; I see it has nothing to learn because I have nothing to teach; I see it as the completed object because I have no subjective reservations whatever, no ideals, preconceptions, preferences, or feelings in the matter. When nothing's in God's heaven, all's right with the world. Now are restored to the universe its own infinite riches; all things are utterly, utterly transfigured, aglow with morning splendour, now that they are where in fact they have always been—over there—and not one of them is here.

Not just a few, but all people are lovable, because I *don't* love them a bit—because there's no love left in Me, and all's out there in them. I *give* them all My love, and they are truly loved; but I am not loving, or feeling, or doing, or being, anything at all. Again, I have not a care in the world: it is the world that is full of care, and takes care of the lot. Once it is laid down for ever, there is no burden, but unimaginable wealth pours out at every seam. Evacuate, let be, enjoy!—what could be simpler? Everything passing from the subjective pole to the objective automatically changes its sign from negative to positive.

Man's world continues to be extremely unsatisfactory, out there and on its own plane. Life and death, renewal and destruction, progress and retrogression, just about balance each other, and no radical improvement is possible. Glossing over the terrible facts, ignoring even one tear or groan, is worse than meaningless talk: it is self-deception of a particularly mean and heartless sort. Man has every reason to complain of a world which has no respect for him whatever. And to try to console him with the notion of a beneficent Providence behind the scenes, whose master plan for the Millennium is slowly working out, is to insult him. There is no evidence for anything of the kind.

No, I'm afraid that only My world is good—because I *face* the facts, and *am* none of them.

* * * * *

Chapter 12

God

His God Is Transcendent: Mine Is Immanent

In theory as a rule, and in practice always, a man's God is transcendent, very much outside and beyond him. *And this is perfectly right.* For the idea of a God lurking *inside* a man is an altogether comic — not to say crazy — notion, posing numerous unanswerable questions. What recognisable form does He take there? What are His distinctive functions? When does He come and when does He go? Is He in all organs equally, and if not, where does He live? Can the pious surgeon or radiologist find clearer traces of Him in Douglas Harding's head or heart than in his kidneys or hair or saliva? No; for any straightforward, candid investigator He is certainly not inside the human body, and must be found in another place if at all.

Here is that other place. At least as plainly as He is absent there, He is present here, taking the place of the human physique that never was here. He isn't in Douglas Harding, but in lieu of Douglas Harding — which is a very different story. This divine cuckoo crowds every fledgling out of the nest: He will have no-one here but Himself; everyone else is banished to the land of Elsewhere, which as a result is very thickly populated indeed. Its other name is the universe — the universe there, of which He is the centre, here.

There is many places, and only *here* is one place. If He were there, in so many things, surely He would be divided against Himself, a pantheon rather than a God. There is only one perfectly unique and indivisible place for Him to be, and that is where I clearly see Him now and always.

So there aren't two modes or aspects of the divine presence. He doesn't have two addresses or run a pair of establishments, one on Earth and inside man and the other in Heaven and outside him. God is simply God and man is simply man: they look quite different and they live quite apart, and really there's no excuse for getting them mixed up. The plain man, who locates God beyond the sky in a land of other-worldly splendour and holiness, is far nearer the truth than the thinker who concocts some heavenly-earthly, divine-human mixture that makes the worst of both worlds. Theologians have every reason to insist upon the absolute distinction between God and man, and the dangerous absurdity of confounding them.

But no man (and certainly not Douglas Harding) can *see* the distinction. Only this Simpleton, Myself, whose Home is Here, is allowed indoors, and in a position to look around. I live here alone in unapproachable glory, and man is more surely excluded from My Presence than if he were a million light-years away.

* * * * *

Chapter 13

The Ordinary

He Is Unique: I Am Commonplace

A man isn't a mere man, but something special. He's what makes him *different* from other men, what distinguishes him—his name, address, parentage, bodily peculiarities, job, personal habits and memories and plans. These are the things that count in his own and others' eyes, and to the extent that he loses them he loses self-respect, individuality, and in the end identity: he's no longer himself. And conversely, what he holds in common with other men—his being, thinghood, life, human anatomy and shape and functions and skills, language, traditions—all this is of no account, though it makes up the essential and indispensable 99.999 per cent of him. In practice, the accidental and unique .001 per cent, which clearly identifies him as that man and no other (thus enabling him to get a birth certificate, job, driving licence, passport, wife, pension, death certificate) is the whole of him: so that you might say a man is only a thousandth part of himself, and little more than a label. If this seems an exaggeration, try congratulating him on his marvellous achievement of existence out of Nothing, on the miracle of his being alive, on his having grown up so lately (and in his own short lifetime) from less-than-wormhood to manhood, on the wonder of his actually being able to see you and hear you, on his ability to probe to the limits of the universe, on his own self-awareness. For all this he takes no credit whatever. It doesn't belong to him alone, therefore he disclaims it. He isn't interested. Nor can he be, and remain quite human.

That's how things are out there in the world of men. Here, they are quite different. I am nothing special, nothing out of the ordinary. I am what everyone is; I have what everyone has. I am what makes all things one and the same, the Genus of every species. I am altogether without distinguishing marks, without name, address, birthday, deathday, possessions, character, history, limitations, qualities of any sort. Just to be at all, without being anything in particular, is enough for Me. Do I possess this or that excellence? Only if all share it. If one poor creature in the universe lacks it, so do I. In other words, what is Here is everywhere and common to all, and what is There is only there and unique. This I can easily check for Myself, as when I see that the one on *that* side of the mirror is distinct from everything else, while the One on *this* side is distinct from nothing else.

Hence the irony. Because I separate Myself from nobody I am one with all, and the All is unique, the Alone. And because Douglas Harding separates himself from everybody, he is one of millions and lost in the crowd. In fact, the only way not to be lost is My way, which is to *be* the crowd. Only He who gives up every distinction remains distinct.

* * * * *

Chapter 14

No Brain

Man Is Mindless: I Am Brainless

Electro-chemical messages are always streaming in to a man's brain from his sense organs, and out from his brain to his muscles, thus enabling him to react appropriately to changes in the environment. Nowhere in this ingoing-outgoing process can be found any intervention by a directing consciousness, a self, a soul, or a mind; nor is there any pressing reason for trying to find either a lodgement or a function for any such entity. Explaining nothing, it would only hamper the honest investigator of human and animal behaviour. All I am justified in saying is that one body is seen to react appropriately to another. It will be time to talk of a man's mind when I see anything of the sort. Meanwhile, if that wonderful engine his brain serves him so admirably, what does he want with a mind anyhow?

In any case, just *what* is this mind or consciousness one is so anxious to credit him with regardless of evidence? I know well what it is, because it is what I am: and it isn't a neat, unobtrusive thing that could be tucked away somewhere in a man's head without upsetting it. Nor is it a harmless and stable substance which would do him no injury, but more like an infinitely corrosive acid, or an infinitely explosive bomb, capable of destroying universes. Then, again, it isn't even itself, but everything but itself... The truth is that it can't be found *anywhere* in the outside world: the world just can't take it. On the contrary, it takes the world, easily and naturally, from this Centre. It fits nowhere but here, and no-one but Me.

One needs a brain *or* a mind, since one cannot have both. For Myself, seeing that I am brainless, I need to be Mind. For I observe, with the utmost clarity and certainty, that there is no nucleus or organ or switchboard or anything else here, and that any influences arriving here come to Nothing, and that any actions proceeding from here come from Nothing, and that this central Nothing nevertheless includes everything—includes this universe which is so bright and clear and nowhere mixed with brains, nowhere occluded or spattered with the flesh-and-blood contents of any little bone box of a head. In short, I see that I am this brainless Mind, of which man's mindless brain is a minute fraction.

And if his mindless brain works wonders, it is because My brainless Mind works *all* wonders, and is in fact the one Mind of all the brains it includes. Ultimately, then, nothing whatever is mindless: it is all Me, and I am all Mind. The real question isn't whether a man, or any other creature, has a mind or not, but where he keeps it. And the answer always is: HERE.

* * * * *

Chapter 15

No Body

Man Is All Body: I Am All Mind

The baby doesn't at first give itself a body, or others a mind; and neither does the Sage. My total lack of body and man's total lack of mind are inseparable sides of one datum: I can't honestly admit the first and deny the second, bowing to only half the evidence. It's no good going by what I see here and refusing to go by what I see there: the presence of his head (his *mere* head, as substantial and unmystical an object as any pumpkin) is no less clearly given than the absence of Mine, and as easily overlooked. In fact, it's just as difficult to exorcise the mind from that head as it is to exorcise the head from this Mind, and no less important.

Man doesn't attempt the task. For him, these little hairy spheres, punctured in seven places, are so bewitched, so haunted, so specially privileged, so charged with Mana, that they are virtually invisible. A man doesn't really *look* at his neighbour: he picks up a few signals and invents all the rest: he no more attends to the presented shapes and textures and colours and movements than he attends to the features of a pouncing tiger. And from this blindness, this substitution of imagination for inspection, proceed all manner of troubles. It is this projected mind, this refusal to take one's neighbour exactly as one finds him, which makes understanding impossible. It generates endless illusion, disappointment, anger, anxiety, jealousy, misery of every kind. Human life is what happens when body and mind are mixed up.

Divine life is what happens when they are separated. Because I am all Mind and no body, and man is all body and no mind, and there is no confusion between us, there is complete understanding. It would be as ridiculous to quarrel with, or love, or hate, or be jealous of, or to blame, or to congratulate, a mere pumpkin-head as to enter into personal relations with the hat it wears. There are no crimes and no virtues in My view: all is conditioned, and understood, and would be forgiven—if there were anyone to receive forgiveness.

What, then, becomes of the divine compassion? There remains no body and no mind outside Me, not a dust-grain that is not altogether Myself. All, therefore, are cared for in the most intimate and thorough fashion conceivable. To the meanest, weakest, worst thing, I say: 'You are Myself'. Is there any sympathy, or gift, to match that? This is not a matter for speculation, but for investigation. Do I, in fact, when I am truly Myself (which means truly Alone) find Myself dismissing any creature with contempt, as a mere illusion, or soulless clod? No! The paradoxical fact is that only then can *nothing* be spared; or despised, or pass unloved.

* * * * *

Chapter 16

The Inanimate

Man Animates: I Kill

Man always brings his surroundings to life. Unfortunately, however, the more life and mind and spirit he attributes to the beings around him the less satisfactory his relations with them become. The immense appeal of sky and stars, of clouds and mountains, of the desert and the open sea, lies in their lifelessnesss: they are sublime, tranquilising, curative, to the degree that they are felt to be inanimate. Forests and fields, trees and flowers and wild creatures, are less pacifying, for mind is already beginning to emerge. As for men, they invariably disturb. Nevertheless social relations may be fairly smooth when they are governed by convention and routine rather than by mind: so long as humans work together according to rules and for limited practical ends—for instance, in the regiment or ship or factory or office—and are content to let each other's private lives alone, they generally get on well enough. Again, where the intenser mental relationships are periodically broken by intense physical ones, as in married life or very dangerous situations, comparative harmony is obtainable.

It is an unhappy fact (but quite natural and inevitable) that human relationships are frequently at their worst where, ostensibly, they should be at their best—at those intellectual and spiritual levels where almost no practical tasks or conventions or privacy or reserves of any sort remain, and mind nakedly confronts mind. Religion is peaceful only when it is either half-hearted or authoritarian. The intenser it becomes, and the freer from traditional forms, the more animosity it generates: imperceptible differences are exaggerated into heresies, and indeed it is the personalities who are most alike (because most advanced) who are apt to clash most violently. The higher the religion the more explosive, till every member is a persecuting sect. And no wonder: the truth is that there's room in the world for any number of bodies, but for only one mind. Minds in the plural become increasingly unworkable and absurd as they achieve more and more the illusion of independence; till in the end the contradictions come to a sudden climax, and the One intervenes.

I am that One, and I live by Myself. I kill, rather than bring to life, My surroundings. I see quite clearly that these wonderfully complex humans are really no more spirits or selves or minds than these poor, inanimate waves and clouds and stars are. I recognise no other self, for aloneness is the hallmark of divinity. And amongst men the furthest from Me is the one who, imagining himself to be a spirit in the highest spiritual company, is of all things the least alone. I am his only Remedy.

* * * * *

Chapter 17

Foolishness

He's Sensible: I'm A Perfect Fool

Ten fools, travelling cross-country together, came to a fast-flowing river, which by one means and another they managed to cross. Arrived on the far bank, each of them counted to make sure all were safely over; and each counted *nine*. So they all began weeping for their drowned brother.

Then a monk came along and, taking pity on them, undertook to prove that all ten were safe. He told them to count the cries of pain while he gave each man one blow with a stick. This time the fools all counted *ten*, and went on their way reassured.

That is the rather lame end of the traditional story, so let us supply a sequel:-

Before the ten ex-fools had got very far, one of them began to have doubts. Returning, he found the helpful monk and said: "True, there were ten cries of pain, but it is *men* that drown, not ouches, and the way to count men is to count heads. And there are still only nine."

At this the monk, realising that he was dealing with a real Fool, and that argument was useless, led him to a part of the river where the water was still and deep.

"There," he cried, pointing down beneath the mirror-smooth surface, "*there* is your tenth fool!"

"We told you so," cried the Fool. "There he lies, our poor drowned brother!" And he began weeping and wailing all over again.

The monk, who was now desperate, raved and shouted back: "You priceless Idiot, it's YOU there in the water, and that's where you deserve to be!"

At this the Fool gave a great laugh and cried: "Hurray, it's only me!" And he ran back to tell his nine companions the good news that everything was all right and it was only he that was drowned. But they had moved on, and he couldn't find them, or anyone else at all, to tell his story to.

He was utterly alone, with not even his drowned self for company.

The moral of this ancient Eastern story, with its modern sequel, is: if you want life and company, don't be a Fool and go by what you see: go by hearsay. *It is not safe to look.*

* * * * *

Chapter 18

Indifference

He Has Feelings: I Have None

As soon as I inspect Myself carefully, I find I have no feelings, pleasant or unpleasant, sublime or commonplace. This Look-out or Observation-post remains unmoved and serene, whatever the turmoil around. I notice that I am never frightened here, or cheerful here, or pleased or loving or hating here; but that, on the contrary, it is the world out there which is frightful, agreeable, lovable, hateful. Right here is no noun for these or any other adjectives to qualify: they refer to the inhabited periphery and never to the vacant Centre. I am characterless.

Savages and young children and some madmen may be said to approach this divine state of central indifference. It isn't they who are horrified but their enemies who are horrifying; it isn't they who suffer from nerves but the world that is menacing and chancy; it isn't they who are in excellent form but other people who are kind and charming. But the difference—and it is crucial—is this: the child attributes no qualities to the Observer because he doesn't see Him, while I attribute no qualities to the Observer because I do see Him. The primitive is unlike Me in that he is pre-psychological and overlooks the Looker, whereas I am non-psychological and always looking at the Looker and finding Him inscrutable.

Psychological man is too sophisticated to do either. Falling between these two stools of Paradise and Heaven, he lands in Hell, where all the world's beauty lies in the beholder's eye, all its meaning in the thinker's head, all its glories and terrors in the human heart. Whereas I am empty of feelings about the splendidly full world, he is full of feelings about the miserably empty world, and continually shaken and tormented by his own likes and dislikes, loves and hates, hopes and fears. The values he has sucked in from the surrounding universe have suffered badly in transit, and leave him no peace. He is more possessed than possessing.

And I have only to look around to see that each man does, in fact, lie at the meeting point of countless influences, both menacing and favourable, which constitute his world, which move him profoundly, which actually become him. Clearly he has no central Observation Tower, no impregnable Keep, but is vulnerable and sensitive through and through.

It hurts to be human. And, of course, to be a perfectly dispassionate man would be monstrously inhuman and out-of-place — if it were possible. His feelings do him credit. What would be the use of his trying to usurp My place and copy Me?

* * * * *

Chapter 19

Asymmetry

Unlike Him, I Am Never One Of A Pair

A man and a woman are out walking together, arm in arm, well matched, on equal terms. The happy exchange of laughter and talk is two-way, the enjoyment mutual. If they stop to kiss, it is lip to lips or to make love, it is man to woman and woman to man. In short, they are a couple, a pair. And this is typical of human relationships: they are symmetrical.

When the Lord God walks in the Garden in the cool of the evening, He is nothing whatever like Adam. He is the Perfect Stranger, in this world but not of it. He sees — I see — that I am never one of a pair, never among equals, never in symmetrical relationship with anything. If I am out walking with My friend, I have only to take us both in, in a sideways glance, to see that only one of us is a human being walking, while the other is more like his guardian angel floating alongside. His talk proceeds from a mouth, Mine from nowhere; he smiles and frowns, I am inscrutable; he is solid, I am ghostly. Our conversation is between a somebody and a nobody, between a body there and a transparency here. We aren't merely different species: we belong to different Kingdoms — he to Earth's Kingdom, I to the Kingdom of Heaven, of which I am indeed the King.

Life with Douglas Harding provides a striking instance of this total incompatibility or one-sidedness: we are indeed an ill-assorted couple. In every sense his very opposite, I am indeed Someone Else, a divine Being here confronting a human being there, with the plate glass mirror parting us more effectively than if it were armour plate. And if I envisage his career—his human birth and death, and all the births and lives and deaths of his immense pre-individual and post-individual history—I remain exempt from it all: I come through every incident untouched. It isn't that I break away from him, or erect any barrier between us, but that I see I can never be involved. For I *face* the total situation: I have before me all Douglas Harding's limitations, all his pains and miseries, his meanness and feebleness, his endless failures, his sloth, his stupidity, his blindness, as well as his more encouraging qualities. And what I *face*, what I confront, is not Me.

I come clean—not that I was ever dirtied with any quality. My Face is permanently unveiled, and so unreserved and frank and open that it never holds back the slightest thing: all's out there in the face opposite. In fact, it's only because *nothing* of him remains here that he has any face to show out there.

* * * * *

Chapter 20

Idleness

Man Acts: I Am Idle

When I attend to what lies here at the storm-centre of the universe, I find perfect calm: the middle of the world has quietly dropped out—or rather, the world never had a middle, but was always hollow, coreless. This Hub of the ever-turning cosmic wheel has never been anything but still, idle, and vacant.

I observe also, radiating like four wobbly spokes from the Hub, this pair of hands and feet going about their own business, just as these men and animals and clouds and sun and stars are going about theirs, without any interference from Me. Here at the Centre I have no aims, no needs, no desires, no responsibilities, no sense of controlling anything whatever: out there all goes well enough on its Own. In any case, how could this Nothing bring any influence to bear upon something, and still itself be Nothing?

The truth is that there are two quite different kinds of limbs—the attached and the loose. Almost all the hands and feet I see around are continuous with some human body (complete with trunk, head, brain) and are evidently going about that human body's business: to look on these appendages as separate creatures would be absurd. It is quite otherwise with these two hands and two feet which I call (or mis-call) 'mine' in the foreground. They are plainly detached from any owner, free from control by any human or animal head and brain, serving no human purpose, and seemingly as free as any other creature out there to behave as they like. Indeed I notice—contrary, perhaps, to expectation—that often their best work is done when I am most aware of their total separation from Me.

I interfere with nothing out there, and nothing out there interferes with Me. I have nothing to do, and yet I see that I am the mainspring of all doing; I find no need to be anything, and yet I see that all being proceeds from Me—from this unique Gap, this Hollowness, which is the fountain of continual creation. In man, on the other hand, no such Gap can be found: he is unbroken, centreless, continuous with all the world, a conductor and not a source of energy; all of him is active as one piece, without any still pivot or nucleus. His very life is action. For him, inaction is death; for Me it is the well-spring of life.

Here is indeed no ordinary spot: there is no place on the map, no place in the entire cosmos, at all like it. This still Centre is the one locality where energy is actually discovered welling up out of Nothing. The inexhaustible energy which flows *through* every other place flows *out of* this Place, without ever ruffling its perfect calm.

* * * * *

Chapter 21

Heaven

It is quite reasonable to suppose (as some children and simple adults do) that God is housed like a God—in Heaven, and not at all like man on earth: in a really wonderful Heaven, having more-than-royal splendour, unique loveliness and charm, and (dare it be said?) all manner of miraculous appointments. Well, if the universe has a King, and that King lives in a Palace at all worthy of Him, what *is* it like?

No man can say: it is hidden from him. But for Me, the King Himself, who is always in residence, it is all plain: I have only to look and see. The actual quality of what I see—the glow, the brilliance, the beauty—is beyond description; and so are the pervading hush, the inner power, the smile, and the peace and joy over all things. Nevertheless some of the grosser and more spectacular features of My Palace may be roughly sketched in without serious distortion. And they are, in fact, just the sort of magical thing a child would delight in. All fairy stories are really incomplete versions of this true Fairy Story.

My Palace, with its gardens and parks, comprises the whole world, but it is a very unfamiliar world indeed. Though the views in all directions are delightful, and often very grand and awe-inspiring, it is not a very vast, or even a well-equipped domain by earthly standards. Its numerous towers and turrets and pavilions and halls are all miniature and bare of furnishings: they are more like toy-theatre scenery than real structures—beautiful, but flat and flimsy facades meant more for show than use.

It is when I visit one of these parts of My Palace that the miracles begin to happen. Everything opens out like a gigantic flower at My approach, and all the goods I might need spring up from nothing, ready-made and well-arranged, around Me: so that My immediate surroundings are always roomy and properly furnished. In some ways these heavenly chairs and tables and carpets and curtains and pictures aren't unlike their earthly counterparts, but they behave quite differently: they are always changing their size and their shape — just as if they were very much alive, and indeed highly observant. Thus a chair, at first no bigger than, say, a pea or a matchbox, obligingly grows to full size as I approach it, stays that size and quite still all the while I'm sitting on it, and quickly dwindles again to matchbox size when I get up and move away. Again, My side of the table is always conveniently wider than the other, but if I move across, the table-top kindly reshapes itself for Me. Again, the patch of carpet I'm standing on has a larger and brighter and more interesting pattern than the rest, a pattern which moves along with Me like a theatre spotlight. Pictures — even Old Masters — paint themselves for Me as I walk up to them; tape-measures lengthen till they've marked themselves off into thirty-six true inches; weights stop growing at exactly an ounce or a pound; printing magnifies to readable size; plates round themselves; coats let themselves out till they fit.

Everything is busy remodelling itself to My convenience. For example, though all the chairs and tables and sofas around Me are queerly and variously distorted — some have only one or two legs apiece, others none — they don't let Me down: all the mis-shapen writhings of My possessions are only a kind of bowing to Me, their sort of worship and obedience, their elaborate preparations for My coming, their careful anticipation of My needs, their reversion to nothing when My needs have been met. To say that I am waited upon by all Heaven is an understatement: here, each brick and tile, each grass blade, each pebble and grain of sand, tirelessly attends upon Me, hangs on My slightest movement, and its response is always perfectly adequate.

A great deal more could be said about the entertainments and conveniences of this wonderful Palace of Mine—how flowers suddenly bloom around Me but nowhere else; how birds sing for Me alone, and are silent when I am gone; how scents and colours revive when I pass by; how rich and fascinating decorations, often set with sparkling jewels, are painted upon surfaces just in time for My arrival, and fade immediately I turn away; how innumerable humans (of all sizes from a fraction of an inch upwards) devote their lives to Me; how I am the end and aim of all that is going on in My Palace of Heaven. Again, it should be explained how, truly speaking, I don't move around Heaven at all, but Heaven moves around Me, who am seated for ever upon My Here-Now Throne at the centre, while Heaven's shows parade before Me; and how, truly speaking, this endless procession of My creatures, of sights and sounds and scents, isn't over there at a distance, but absolutely one-with-Me, here.

In fact, however, all these magical displays and appointments are merely incidental to heavenly life. The King is certainly well aware of His enchanting Palace, but only by the way, as part of His Self-awareness. Really it is Himself alone that He sees—Himself the indescribable Light of Heaven, the unfathomably Mysterious and Wonderful One, the Solitary One, the Only One—and Heaven is (so to say) a by-product of that seeing. Heaven is *where* I am when I am concerned only with *what* I am. That is why it is no nebulous

Mansion in the sky, but much more real—yes, more real in its concrete detail—than any place on earth. This Fairyland is the true Fatherland, and man's world is only a fantastic dream.

* * * * *

Chapter 22

The Universe

His World Is Real, Mine Unreal

A man had better take the universe seriously — or suffer the consequences. For plainly he's of a piece with it, built into the same block, a current of the same onrushing river. His dependence upon and continuity with the world are total: not for an instant can he be disentangled. Through and through he's of the same order as the things and processes around him, and is exactly as real — and as unreal — as they are. To him, therefore, reality means the natural world in all its vastness and energy and variety — a world in which consciousness is (at best) a late and rare accident, altogether feeble and insignificant if not actually a myth. And a cool look at him is enough to confirm that his consciousness is not a necessary hypothesis.

When I observe Myself all is reversed. No matter, no complications, not even naked energy is here, but only awareness of Awareness itself, immediate Self-Consciousness, that ever-simple Reality which the universe — its incidental by-product — can never stain or disturb.

I cannot take the universe seriously. Deep down, I feel it's not my native country and I don't belong. Also I see clearly that I'm not remotely like any of its inhabitants. Moreover I — and I alone — have the art of exposing its emptiness and dreamlike unreality. Just as easily as I clear up here all that fantastically complex opacity of cells and tissues and organs which build a human body, so I clear up all the rest of the world, from the furniture of this room to the furthest galaxy. At will and effortlessly, I put all things behind Me and so abolish them. Not only do I awake from the daydream of the universe every night, but as often during the day as I wish. I'm the lightest of sleepers. In fact, I'm not Myself till I am wide awake, which means awake to Myself alone.

To survive the universe, one must undo it down to the last atom, for to allow it any reality is to share its fate. Unlike men, I'm not taken in by the world-hoax: I take it in and see through it and make Nothing of it. I've never been in the world: nor, truly speaking, has it ever been in Me. In Me is only Myself, and the whole creation melts instantly, now, without a tell-tale bubble or swirl, into this clear Ocean.

* * * * *

Chapter 23

Advertisements

Advertisements And Invertisements

The adman's skill largely consists in persuading the beholder to put himself in the picture, so that he becomes unconsciously identified with the main figure in the advertisement. In the wise and good father inquiring about family insurance, in the hypochondriac looking for new symptoms and their cures, in the mother preening herself on the whiteness of her little girl's nightdress, in the tweedy young man at the wheel of his sports car, in the super-elegant wearer of hats or coats or shoes, the potential buyer recognises himself or herself, and responds appropriately. "That's me!" is the unconscious reaction to the successful poster; and if the face on the hoarding is handsomer, and the figure younger, and the setting more expensive than in real life, so much the better for business.

If I am not taken in by these advertisements it is because I don't see Myself in them. I am out of the picture. What, indeed, have these human faces to do with the Faceless One?

The adman, however, is not defeated. He has other designs, of a very different kind, which are directed at Me—they might be called invertisements. They are portraits, not of men and women and children, but of missing persons, of bodies that have (except for odd hands and feet) disappeared. A favourite poster—it certainly doesn't *look* like a holy icon, though that's in fact what it is—shows Me raising a spoon or a glass or a cigarette towards this no-mouth and no-head, this 'hole where a head should have been'. And the fact that I accept these bizarre portraits of Me as true likenesses without thinking them odd, without thinking about them at all, shows how accurate they are.

It is much the same with films: there are two very different sorts — the human sort, and My sort. In the former, the hero is a human being, with whom the cinema audience has no difficulty in identifying itself. In the latter, the hero is not a human being at all, but a void or transparency, a disembodied voice, the sound of hard breathing and occasional coughs, loose hands fiddling with pipe or matches or spectacles or pen, loose feet shuffling in and out at the bottom of the screen — in short, a film portrait of Me. The former shows a human being coming and going, ever changing, always off-centre to the world; the latter shows this divine being fixed, unchanging, at the world's empty centre.

And again, this strange picture seems perfectly natural, because it is Me to the life.

* * * * *

Chapter 24

Subjectivity

Man Is Object: I Am Subject

I see that I am a subject and never an object—never a man, or any other thing, but the empty receptacle of everything, of all objects, including the one called Douglas Harding. Among these objects themselves I can find no trace of subjectivity: they are presented as objects pure and simple. Thus a man is visibly a physical thing which is separate from other physical things; he shows no sign of melting or exploding into the universe, or of concealing it somewhere on his person. In short, he is a minute part, and how could even the greatest of parts contain the whole?

It is true that frequent attempts are made to confer upon him subjectivity of some sort. Since he evidently neither comprises nor owns *this* universe, he is credited with another, a private or pocket universe, which mysteriously copies the first. The problem is where to put this additional universe. One solution is to shrink it to manageable size and enclose it in a captive balloon floating just above the man's head. But this balloon-world rarely appears outside cartoons and comic strips, and is not to be taken too seriously. A more respectable—but perhaps still less likely—position for this second universe is not above but right inside the man's skull. This means even more drastic shrinkage, and confinement in a tiny, dark, and airless box which is already stuffed full. It is not explained how this boundless, huge, luminous, brilliantly coloured, full-scale, and dangerous world could be all safely folded up and tucked away in such a tiny container as a head, without bursting it, and itself turning into something quite different; or how this miracle of universe-shrinking (or else head-swelling) is renewed every time another head appears in the world. Nor is it explained why no surgeon working on the brain has ever come across any trace of a miniature universe lurking there. The truth is that this second universe—whether stuffed into or floating above a man's head—is a dream and an absurdity. The myriad objects comprise this *one* world—immense, luminous and full-scale—presented to this *one* Subject.

And man is of one sort: he takes only the headed form, as I take only the headless. I notice this suits him well enough, and I have no plans to behead him or cram his head full of foreign matter. This is not to say that he inhabits some outer darkness unlit by consciousness. He doesn't lack a Subject, namely Myself. I am the unique Subject, Centre, Self and Knower of all objects, and if any claim subjectivity it is Mine they claim. All heads share this No-head. Though I am pure Subject and they are pure objects, all are Me, and in reality beyond any such distinctions.

* * * * *

Chapter 25

The Face

His Face Is Human: Mine Is Divine

It is evening. Calm and relaxed, shedding the burden of the day's prejudices and preconceptions, prepared for anything, I begin to take stock of the situation as it presents itself at this moment. I settle down to comparing what is sitting in this easy chair with what is sitting in that one opposite.

In *that* chair, two yards away, sits a human being. In *this* chair sits (at most) only half a human being—and the bottom half at that. Crowning *that* chair is a 'face'—a kind of grey-pink bladder curiously ridged and furrowed and blotched, punctured in several places, and set in a fringe or mat of brown hairs. Crowning *this* chair is nothing of the sort—no pinkness, no punctures, no hairs. How unlike are the occupants of these two easy chairs!

I go on studying that pinkish balloon six feet off. How small and dull it is, how closed in upon itself, how stand-offish and parted from other things, how tight and opaque, how tiresome a gadget to be tied to for life: and how it contrasts with this unbounded, weightless, self-luminous transparency here! How clear is My complexion, how frank and open My expression, how alert and penetrating My gaze! It is as if this Face were one broad smile with no features to frame it, or a single Eye so deep and limpid that it is eternally invisible, or a Yawn so wide that it has yawned the top half of its body away.

How serene and immobile is this Face, how ageless and unmarked by time and sadness! Here, indeed, is the divinely calm Face, the Face of incomparable freshness and brilliance, the Face of eternal youth, the lovely shining Face of God Himself. And all around its rocklike placidity surges the great sea of little human faces—all different, all agitated and marked with suffering, all dying. Nevertheless this Face is anything but aloof from them: on the contrary, it is so friendly, so unveiled and open, that it includes all faces. In fact, it sees itself in and through them at one glance, and never alongside them. Each human face is only itself and excludes all the others: this Face *is* all the others. Man's face may detect the world: Mine *is* the world.

When I stare at the clear sky my Face is blued; at night it blackens; in a garden it is made up with the brightest paints and powders, upon no base whatever; confronting My friend in the easy chair opposite, it is exquisitely human. As I contemplate that dear face I notice that there is on *this* side of it nothing whatever—no seer, no physiognomy, no viewpoint even. I have no Face now but his. Every face is the divine Face when God sees it. And who else does see it?

No wonder early pictures of the Buddha show an *empty* seat.

* * * * *

Chapter 26

Hands

Those Hands Are Man's: These Are God's

The human hand, if it is at all alive, invariably adheres to a human body; and it is usually busy at some task of exploration or grasping or manipulation designed to promote the interests of its human user. This is not to say that the human hand is understood in the slightest: it is only familiar.

God's hand, though no more mysterious, is a less commonplace object. It figures in certain mediaeval paintings, where it looks just like a man's hand, with wrist and a short length of sleeve, except that it fades away at that point and is attached to no body. Making some appropriate gesture, it is thrust forth from a cloud—or from a pattern of celestial spheres, or from nothing—commonly situated at the top right-hand corner of the picture.

So far from being a mere iconographical curiosity, this pious device is, in fact, a fairly true picture of *these* hands—of the hand that is now writing these words, and the other that is holding down this sheet of paper. I see that, though they are very much alive, yet they are quite loose and joined to no body, but fade out around the elbows. They proceed from, and die away into, the void that lies just back of them—this Void which is Me. They are God's hands, the only living hands I have ever seen that belong to no man, to nobody but Him.

Certainly they aren't Douglas Harding's, for here is no solid human trunk for them to be directed by or to serve, but only this divinely vacuous Trunk which has no lack, no desires, no future, and therefore no tasks of its own for any hands to undertake. It is true that I am aware of their astonishing behaviour and authorise it all, but I am in every sense detached alike from their action and its results. They live their own life. I am not now laboriously directing this right hand: nimbly, mysteriously, wonderfully, it writes these words about itself as it pleases — and I am neither pleased nor displeased. Moreover, I notice that when I see quite clearly Who I am here, I see also that these two hands aren't attending to Douglas Harding's affairs, but display diviner powers, a new selflessness, a surer touch, an unfamiliar spontaneity and freedom.

In the last resort of course, *all* hands, all limbs whatever, are Mine. Innumerable and ramifying in all directions, they nevertheless all branch out of this slender central Trunk, and handle My business everywhere. The universe is My Body, and the whole of it is ranged region by region, not around any human nucleus, but around the divine Emptiness here, lurking just behind these two five-fingered Mysteries.

* * * * *

Chapter 27

Love

Divine Love And Human Love

Divine love is a kind of dying. Only as abolished—as Nothing—can I love anyone unreservedly. Only when every defence here has been smashed, and all obstructing thoughts and feelings and judgments have been swept away, do I keep open house, and become perfectly hospitable and loving. The mark of this divine charity is that it is unbounded and undiscriminating, as freely poured out upon the mean and ugly as upon the most deserving. It has nothing to do with sentiment or convention or morality, and is always the same. It cannot be produced to order or cultivated, but occurs naturally when I really see what I am—namely, this self-luminous Emptiness here, which obviously has nothing to lose, gain, fear, or hope for. This Love is (so to say) an inevitable by-product of this Seeing, of this Clear Light in which all things shine. God is Love because He is Light—not that they can really be separated. .

Unlike Me, man is neither empty nor nothing. He is a very definite something—something picked out and shown up by My Light, and not that insubstantial Light itself. Quite obviously, he excludes other things: his being a body means that he crowds out all other bodies from the space he occupies; he stands in their way and is necessarily inhospitable. His love, therefore, is very different from Mine: it is attraction and attachment to another like himself, a bond which links lover and loved one without invading or destroying either:

indeed it is a love which insists that the lover shall be fully himself and as alive as possible. Also it is extremely partial. A man has only a limited amount of love to bestow, and a limited field over which to spread it — he can't get close to everyone — so it is his children and near relations, his particular friends, his native city and country and race, and his own heavenly body, that he loves best, or loves at all. If his love is real and not just vague sentiment, the nearest is for him always the dearest.

For Me, however, there is neither near nor far (I do not see distance) and all are equally dear. All are Myself, inasmuch as My nothingness involves, or rather is, their somethingness. They have no separate existence, yet every one of them is needed to fill this great empty Heart of Mine.

As extreme heat is easily mistaken for extreme cold, so extreme love is easily mistaken for extreme indifference; and indeed there are resemblances. If I seem cold, it is through excess of heat. But the only way to know My love is to be Me, and exercise it.

* * * * *

Chapter 28

The Seen

Unlike Man, I Am Clearly Visible

The notion that God must take on human form, if He is to be seen at all, couldn't be further from the truth. He alone is perfectly visible, and man is almost perfectly invisible.

Nobody ever really sees a man, but only catches fleeting glimpses of something that hints at him. Even if you now have him before you, in a good light and in full front view, much of that front view is foreshortened and distorted by perspective, and his sides and back are missing, and so are his insides, and so are his past history and future destiny, and so are the worldwide relationships which make him what he is. What you are really seeing is part of a coloured surface, lacking any depth in time and space, and no man at all. Like every other thing, he is invisible, and indeed unknowable. For to take in all of him, and know him thoroughly, would be to take in all his aspects and all that conditions them, which is to say the universe itself. In other words, man is a product of ignorance: it is his very nature to be obscure and mysterious. If you know very much about him it is no longer him you know, but something much greater; and if you were to know all about him you would have to know all things everywhere and at all times, and as man he would have vanished altogether.

Only I can be completely seen, known, and understood beyond all possibility of error. For I alone am this perfectly pure transparency which is free from every difference and complication, from every trick of perspective in space and time, from all history—but nevertheless brilliantly self~luminous, obvious, unavoidable. If this Clear Void which I am is seen at all it is seen clearly, and it's impossible just to take a peep at Me, or glimpse Me through a haze. Nor can I be seen now without being seen for ever and ever, exactly as I always am, complete and unchanging.

It is true that I am hidden from outsiders. If the pure in heart shall see God, that is only because the pure heart *is* God. I am to be seen only here, by one who coincides with Me, and who is indeed none other than Myself: and this is the guarantee that I am seen truly. All other objects are seen falsely, because the seer is remote from the seen, and out of touch with what he really is. For instance, a man's hair is brown and shiny only at a distance: close up, it is neither, nor is it even hair. Only in My case do appearance and reality merge and become identical. *Only I am what I look like.*

What am I? is easy. *What is he?*—that is the hard, the unanswerable question. There can be no inside information of anyone but God. Man is known *about*; I alone am known.

* * * * *

Chapter 29

Centrality

He Is Off-Centre: I Am The Centre

Nothing is for Me as it is for Douglas Harding. It isn't that he lives in a very different *world* (why multiply universes unnecessarily?) but in a very different *place* in the world: I am established at this unique Centre of all things, while he hangs around somewhere on the outside. And, after all, this critical difference of situation—with its huge consequences for us both—is as natural as it is obvious. How could any mere man, whom I see to be only one of countless others like him (and he readily admits it) claim to be the Hub of the universe? Only the unique One, Myself, who can find none that at all resembles Me, has any right to such a station.

However, it's not so much a question of qualifications for the post as of looking to see what it's like to occupy it: and a glance out at My world at once shows how wonderfully it is all organised around this Centre. Wherever I go in the world, however fast I travel, I never leave this Place: in fact, it is the world that is always on the move and readjusting itself around Me—I just stay here and let it sort itself out. For example, if a large crowd of men are admitted into My Presence, their bodies shrink—some to the size of toy soldiers and even smaller—till all are got in. The narrow lane widens. specially for Me, closing in again after; tiny flowers grow big around Me, colours sparkle and brighten, music gathers volume where I am. If it is sun and mountains and meadows and chalets and flowers that I am enjoying all at once, then each leaves room for the others, and I see that the sun is no bigger than the sunflower, and the mountain may be smaller than the cottage or the cow—all to My convenience. Again, I note that the sun and the moon, all the stars, and even galaxies, rotate about Me; and so do terrestrial things, though more erratically. They know their place, and have infinite respect for Mine. And if any dare to come too near, My divine power slays them and consumes them utterly. All things fit themselves to Me alone, totally ignoring others. At every instant, the whole world bows to Me: it just can't help doing so.

How very unlike Me is man! I see objects approach and touch him without even being damaged, and recede from him without shrinking; I see that they neither adjust their sizes to his convenience nor circulate about him. It isn't that the world pays no attention to him, but that it does just what it likes with him, fitting him to Me, and ensuring that his respect for this One Centre is unwavering and unquestioning. It is the nature of the universe that it cannot do with two Centres, and that the rule of the One is absolute.

* * * * *

Chapter 30

Education

Education Is Retreat From Me

Education is a long and painful cutting down to size. It is making sure that young Douglas grows up into a man amongst men — that is to say, into something as unlike Me as possible. All his early tendencies in My direction, all his crude attempts to keep himself at the Centre of things, are patiently discouraged, till in the end he is quite happy to be one of many millions and truly human.

He learns, for instance, that he is really the same shape as the creatures around him and there is a top half to his body; that his feet are really bigger than his hands; that houses which look small aren't dolls' houses, that trees which look small aren't bushes, that mountains which look small aren't hillocks, but that these things are only distant; that all railway lines are really parallel and most rooms rectangular; that even remote cities can be important and ancient empires great; that the Earth isn't a platform at the centre of the universe, but a relatively tiny sphere cavorting round an undistinguished star; and so on. All these, and countless other items of practical — indeed, indispensable — human knowledge, take the growing child further and further from his primitive self-centredness into that realm of centreless objectivity where he truly belongs; for to be a man at all is to be one piece — no more — in an immense jigsaw puzzle, and to fit snugly into the pattern in which no piece dominates.

There is nothing wrong with this. The proper business

of education is to turn infants into the best sort of human beings and not into divine beings of any sort whatever. It must lead away from Me. The more cultivated the mind, the less Godlike.

For I am mindless. I see the world naively from this Centre alone, without benefit of education, with no practical axes to grind, with no reputation for modesty to keep up, with no intentions or plans, with no thoughts at all about it. As pure Subject, I am perfectly uncritical, perfectly hospitable to every object exactly as it presents itself—and this includes all the useful conventions and educated inventions which go to make up human Nature. Oddly enough, though it is the professed goal of education to enable men to overcome all personal bias and see things objectively, as they really are, it is only I, the ineducable, who succeed, because only I am content to leave them alone. The ultimate Subjectivity is the ultimate Objectivity.

* * * * *

Chapter 31

Novelty

He Is Old: I Am New

Douglas Harding is a kind of sediment, a vast accumulation, layer upon layer, of racial and individual deposits. He is essentially a preserver, a time-binder, who can never live down his immense past—because he *is* that past. Deprive him of his history, and he is no more. The whole of him is a living fossil, a museum of the past: his body and its extensions in the form of clothes and tools and buildings and cities, his language and social heritage in general, his ever-growing fund of experience functioning as memory and habit and built-in skills—this immense human edifice is its own past surviving in the present. Just as a symphony isn't a symphony in less than half an hour, so man isn't man in less than some thousands and millions of years. He is memory. He is what he *was*.

I am what I *am*. I find that the only way I can see Myself at all is to see Myself afresh at this moment, without memory or any carry-over from the past—not *as if* for the first time, but *actually* so, with all the surprise and delight of new discovery. I notice that if I am truly Self-aware at this moment, I am prepared to find just anything here—a flame, a light, a cloud, a dial or a whole dashboard of dials, machinery, blood, fat, anything at all, however improbable or ridiculous—and if, instead, I *count on* finding here no head, no body, Nothing, the Clear Light of the Void, or God Almighty, I only lose them. I cannot remember having been God, because in fact

I never *was* God. God is God and I am God now and only now, at this very instant. He is *seen*, and all seeing is seeing *now*. He is seen and not remembered: man is remembered and not seen.

Unlike man, I am not to be relied upon. I always come as an astonishment to Myself, as the world's newest and latest Wonder, and can never begin to take Myself for granted. I learn nothing about Myself, never get used to Myself, am always introducing Myself to Myself, bowing with profound respect and the keenest delight at this strange meeting. And this fresh introduction is no mere formality: I truly am brand new, without history, inheritance, continuity of any kind. Every moment sees Me starting from scratch.

Man has much to fall back on. It is his indispensable role to be a hoarder, a capitalist with a large and growing deposit account in the human savings bank, yielding a high rate of interest. But I am naked and poor, without a penny or a pocket to slip it in. I haven't acquired the saving habit—even to the extent of saving Myself.

* * * * *

Chapter 32

Allness

I Am All: Man Isn't Even Himself

What do I add up to? What do I really comprise? There's no-one to refer to: I can only look and see.

I am what I coincide with, what I am not against or alongside or parted from in any way. I am everything which is clearly present here and now in Me, and not absent by so much as a hair's-breadth or an instant. If absolutely nothing comes between you and Me, if no interval of space or time separates us, then you are Myself. And if, to clinch the deal, I have nothing of My own here to put up to you or to put up against you, no contribution to make or influence to exert, why then you are doubly, trebly, infinitely Me!

Directly I look at you, at anything at all, I see that these conditions are perfectly satisfied. No distance comes between that star and Me, between that man and Me, between that hand and Me: however hard and long I stare, I can make out no interval. All those frustrating light-years and parsecs, those miles and feet and inches and hundredths of an inch, are here quite imaginary: every measuring rod stretching between Me and these My objects lies end-on and reduces to a point. The North Star sparkling in the black sky is no further away than the windowpane and these spectacles. Nothing in the universe stands aloof from Me.

It isn't that the star is hard up against Me or superimposed upon Me: there's no eye here to bump into or face to brush. These stars and clouds and mountains and men are evidently content to stay here without anything to hold them in place or contain them: they are simply present as they are, without any fuss or meddling. I am these things because I am nothing else. If I were so much as an atom Myself, that would be enough to hold them all off. It is only the Emptiness which is Full.

What, then, is man? Again, he is that which coincides with him, which is parted from him by no intervening object (however small) or gap. Evidently, in that case, he isn't that star or mountain or man or hand he happens to be looking at: the gap between observer and observed couldn't be plainer. He's only himself—if that. For each limb is visibly and measurably remote from every other, each feature in its own place: nowhere in him is there self-coincidence: all is scattered, exploded. His hand is further from his head than the remotest star is from My No-head. Thus My Universe-body is much more intimately Mine than a man's little body is his. Distant in every part from himself, he isn't really himself. Coinciding in every part with Me, he is Me, and I am all things.

* * * * *

Chapter 33

Creation

He Is Creature: I Am Creator

God brings all things forth from Nothing; or rather, He is that Nothing itself, that empty Womb from which all creatures are born. And I am none other than He (I am He as soon as I take the trouble to notice the fact, and rely solely on what I can see for Myself); and man, including Douglas Harding, is just one of My endless succession of creations. Equally, I am the Destroyer, the same Nothing absorbing and utterly annihilating its own creatures—including, again, Douglas Harding, who is himself quite powerless either to create or destroy a speck of dust. Man lives by remodelling slightly what already exists.

The contrast between us here, as in everything else, is infinitely great. I cause darkness to descend, and dissolve heaven and earth: he only closes his eyes. I command: 'Let there be light!' and create heaven and earth from Nothing: he only opens his eyes. I amputate and destroy these arms and legs: he only raises his head. I re-grow and graft them on again: he only lowers his head. I wipe out that group of men without leaving a trace: he only turns his back. I recreate them entire: he only turns round again. I cheer the whole world up: he only smiles. I calm the whole world: he only takes a pill. I bring forth and abolish many strange worlds: he only stirs and mutters in his sleep. I absorb and so pacify the huge mass of this planet, effortlessly, leaving not a leaf or a stone opaque and unmelted (to say nothing of clearing up all Earth's wars, crises, disasters, crimes): he merely looks up at the Moon. I take in and make Nothing of the great Universe itself: and what he does is simply look into the empty sky—no more. In all these instances, while he is changing himself a little, I am changing the world utterly.

God doesn't think He exercises these divine powers: He *sees* their operation. I actually see the world being made and unmade instantly at My pleasure, and see that none of My creatures has the beginnings of this faculty. A man cannot even add to or subtract from his own little body.

It is an overwhelming experience to find that one is God Almighty, Creator of Heaven and Earth, the Saviour of the World, the Pacification of all things. At the same time it feels quite natural to exercise these tremendous powers, to perform all the while these astounding miracles. It is ludicrously simple and easier than winking, for there is no eye here, no body, no mind, but only simplicity itself and divine ease. Nothing could be more straight-forward and effortless and obvious than My work of Creation; and that is why it is hidden from man, who at all costs must complicate what is given him. It is his business *never* to trust the data.

* * * * *

Chapter 34

Satisfaction

Man Is Restless And Grasping:
I Alone Am Satisfied

I am full-grown, complete, permanently content, for there's nothing I don't possess, or that is still outside Me. How else, indeed, could I have—or want to have—these stars and sun and moon, earth and men and all creatures, for My very own, but precisely the way I have them now? The goods themselves could scarcely be more interesting and glorious, or more surprising and various and prolific; and I cannot reasonably complain that I have still to take delivery of them. Would my ownership be more secure if they were all to come nearer so that I might handle them, or if I were to write My name on them, or somehow fence them in, or get them legally conveyed to Me? Can they get away from Me, escaping beyond the universe? Is their Cage unbarred? Or are they ill-appointed, arranged without taste or imagination? Would I prefer insects in the sky and stars in the garden, tables and chairs on the horizon and mountains and glaciers in the sitting room? Just to ask such silly questions is to see the truth: I am quite satisfied. I have everything, and I have it the way I want it.

How unlike man! Even a world-emperor claims no more than a particle of My empire, and cannot hold that for long, or really hold it at all. To be a man is to be almost nothing trying hard to be something. He wants to grow, to accumulate, but the more successful he is the less satisfied. He is at once too small and too big to be happy—too small, because all that's outside is threatening; and too big, because all that's inside is threatened, an anxiety to hold and maintain.

I alone am content, because I am all things and so have nothing to gain, and because I am Nothing and so have nothing to lose. To expect man to imitate this divine content would expect him to be much less and much more than a man — which is absurd. His restlessness and acquisitiveness are essential ingredients of his human nature, and without his share of them he would be just tired, and certainly no nearer divinity. To take on a head is to take on headaches — responsibilities, troubles, burdens. The penalty for being somebody is that one is neither nobody and therefore free, nor everybody and therefore satisfied. More briefly, the trouble with man is that he isn't Me.

And the end of all his troubles, the salvation of all that is not Me, is the fact that, in reality, all *is* Me. For there is nothing outside Me, nor is there anything inside Me that isn't Me.

* * * * *

Chapter 35

Emptiness

Man Is Full: I Am Empty

I don't care what anyone says: it's a fact that I have never for a moment believed that I have any insides. I observe pieces of bread-and-butter and cups of tea disappearing at one end, and faeces and urine appearing at the other, and between them no oesophagus, stomach, intestines, and the rest, but only emptiness. The bread isn't digested, or vaporised, or atomised, but totally destroyed: it just melts away into Nothing. The faeces don't come out of a container, but emerge, newly created, from the Void; and truly I *make* water. However hard I try, I cannot take very seriously those fascinating anatomical diagrams, those highly coloured wall-pictures of men and women nonchalantly displaying their exploded interiors, their hidden fantastic worlds of organs and tissues more strange and complex than any scenery outside. To men and animals over there they no doubt apply, but not at all to Me here, not to this Hollow One. Others are as replete with anatomies as they claim to be, are solid and substantial, filled out skin-tight with the indispensable apparatus of animal life; I alone am empty, yet alive — alive, it would seem, on quite a different principle and with quite another life. This is what I discover when I pay no attention to books or hearsay, and rely upon what I observe for Myself.

To speak more generally, some part (small or vast) of the world is *here* and not there; and what is *here* is Me; and what is Me is empty — perfectly unified, simple, and transparent. I am the infinitely elastic Core, the infinitely capacious Central Cavity, of the Universe, from which it all emerges and into which it all vanishes. When I speak of France, it is as England rather than as an Englishman that I speak—but an England that is one and void and no longer England. When I look up at Mars, I see that I am seeing for Earth, and feel that I am feeling for Earth—but an Earth that is reduced to pure space, dissolved to the last stone and drop of water. When I look into the empty sky, I am the Universe looking, and the Universe is empty too: there is one clear sky which is neither inside nor outside.

I don't feel any heavier, or more replete, or bigger, as I grow, but rather the reverse. However much or little I take on here, I am unclouded, clearer than glass. All the world's daunting opacity, its terrifying populousness and complexity, the brute stubbornness of its detail—all this melts away the instant I incorporate it. This is the true seeing through the world-illusion. One is no longer taken in by the seeming solidity of things, but instead takes them in—right into this divine Simplicity which lies at the heart of the world. I am the universal Glazier, the Polisher of the World-gem, the Great Clarification. I see through the world. There's Nothing in it.

* * * * *

Chapter 36

Opinions

Unlike Man, I Hold No Opinions

I could differ from you only if I were something Myself. What patiently refuses to put up any resistance, to have anything of its own, is entirely vulnerable to you, entirely in agreement: colourless, it is coloured by you; featureless, it is assimilated to you. I really take in that before which I am nothing. This is the divine open-mindedness which is also no-mindedness. I adhere to no sect or class or party. A good Listener, I have nothing to teach, no advice to give, no judgments to pronounce: I keep My mouth shut, and this is easy because I have none to open. I am wise only in the sense that I reject no-one's wisdom. Like the brainless employer who is nevertheless clever enough to engage the best brains going and make a huge fortune out of them, My infinite wealth of knowledge and savoir-faire isn't really Mine at all. Rejecting no opinions and having none of My own, I *hold* all opinions without distorting any, and positively revel in their clashing contradictions—for example, those which fill this book. My taste is absolutely catholic.

A true man cannot afford such impartiality. He cannot for long sit on the fence, but must presently come down on one side or the other, voting for one party, attending one church, marrying one woman, playing one game well, following one profession, preferring this particular doctrine, book, picture, symphony, country, man, to that one. To refuse such limitation, to insist on remaining perfectly broadminded and uncommitted, is not to be more but less than human. Often it is his duty to advise, to teach, to warn, to condemn utterly: for a man must be true to himself, be known for what he is, and stand by it.

This is both fine and inevitable, but the cost is high: it means living in great discomfort, in a man-made, artificial universe. Necessarily, man sees everything through distorting and coloured human spectacles, adding his own arbitrary interpretations to the data and subtracting all that fails to interest him. Thus, men and animals and plants and things are good or bad according to whether they fit into his plans or upset them. Again, objects are beautiful or ugly by convention — all sunsets, trees overhanging water, garden flowers, and nubile girls are beautiful, while all wounds, sores, decaying things, litter, and filth are ugly. "There's nothing good or bad but thinking makes it so" — and to think is human.

Not to think is divine — not to divide the true from the false, the good from the bad, the beautiful from the ugly, but to take everything just as it's given, here and now, in all innocence, and with open heart and mind. This is seeing the world as it is — utterly transfigured, shining with a Beauty that is beyond beauty and ugliness, and a Goodness that is beyond goodness and evil.

* * * * *

Chapter 37

Presence

Man Is There: God Is Here

God can never be there and man can never be here: *this* is God's place and *that* is man's. I can never get to man's place, because it retreats at My approach; nor can I ever get away from My place, because it keeps up with Me wherever I go. In other words, man is an illusion: when I go looking for him in the place where he seems to be, I find there only Myself. He is always elsewhere, playing at hide-and-seek with himself, a divided personality. I alone am altogether present exactly where I am, Self-coinciding and Self-contained. Man never catches up with himself: he can only be observed as absent, because he is essentially an absentee. I can only be observed as present, because I am essentially on the spot.

In man there is an inherent absurdity, almost a madness: in so far as he exists at all he is beside himself, unable to pull himself together, not all there; and this immense disability he shares with all created things. I alone am all here, at Home to Myself, undivided into subject and object or observer and observed; one part of Me doesn't hold the rest at arm's length to look at it, nor do I surround Myself with real or imaginary observers in order to see Myself through their eyes. I see Myself, not here from there, but here from here, with perfect clarity and with no possibility of distortion by distance, or any tricks of perspective, or inadequate means of communication. This is the only true seeing, infallible, clear, total, when seer and seen are one and in exactly the same place, namely *here*:

and all other seeing, when the seer is remote from the seen (and therefore in no position to say what the seen is *really* like) is only a kind of mis-seeing. In fact, all things there are fakes, pretending to be something they aren't, and only I am *what* I seem, *where* I seem. Strictly speaking, Douglas Harding is nobody and nowhere: he exists in much the same way as mirages and dreams and optical illusions exist. He is not himself. Deprive him of the room to stand away from himself, bring the two halves of him together, and he vanishes.

This is not, however, the end of the story. Looking again, I clearly see Douglas Harding and all men and all things for what they are — mere appearances over there — and Myself for what I am — Reality right here — and so I am in a position to enjoy everything to the full. It is because that world of make-believe there cannot affect the real world here, that it is enjoyable, and indeed perfect. It is also, paradoxically, not alien at all, but utterly one with Me. For in the end, *there* itself is illusory. All things are wholly present in Me, and no distance parts us. I see that *this* side of My objects is — Nothing whatever.

* * * * *

Chapter 38

Home

Man's Out: God's In

If one's in Paris and interested in the Mona Lisa, one doesn't go round asking *what* she's like, but *where* she's to be seen, and the quickest way there. Similarly, if I'm serious about Myself, I track Myself down, locate Myself, come to Myself. I don't waste time collecting third-hand impressions of Me *there* where I never was, from rank outsiders; I call on Myself *here*. And I go on knocking and ringing till I get an answer, because I can be sure of finding Myself in.

Man's always out. He lives a mysterious life in a wholly ungetatable country called Over There, the Yonder Land whose very wretchedness is inaccessible. He doesn't know where the hell he is, but it's hell all right. Hell is there, and *There* is bondage, misery, darkness, limitation, pain, sorrow, death — always next-door-but — one, always in the offing and never brought right home to oneself. In contrast, Heaven is here, and Here is freedom from all limitation, all suffering, all decay. This is indeed the firm ground of optimism — that evil won't bear close inspection. It's dislocated. It's out. And the first thing is to see it there.

Enlightenment's a two-stage spring-cleaning: a good turn-out, then everything back again, all polished and sweet-smelling. First, this body-mind with all its functions and contents, down to the heaviest and oldest piece of inherited furniture, must be got out of Here and stowed over There, leaving this Room absolutely empty. All feeling and perceiving and thinking and willing, along with all things felt and perceived and thought and willed, must be *seen out*, till not a speck of psycho-physical dust can find a hiding-place Here. Only when I'm satisfied this Room is nothing but room, is it ready to take the furniture back again — and then it's not the evil-smelling, faded, worm-eaten, tatty old objects that went out, but everything marvellously dry-cleaned and richly dyed and better than new. In fact, it's this lovely Room itself, so pleasant and commodious and light and fresh and airy, which *makes* its furniture, high-lighting it to perfection; and equally it's this renovated furniture which brings out all the Room's spacious splendour. But really they're inseparable, and so are the two stages of their refurbishing. It's always a gloriously sunny April morning Here, with the spring-cleaning just this instant done, and nothing missing as a result. All's present and infinitely correct, and I'm Home.

* * * * *

Chapter 39

Freedom

Man Is Bound: I Alone Am Free

What is true freedom? It is to contain all that one needs, to be subject to no outside influence, to have everything one's own way, to be perfectly self-sufficient, to be really gay and carefree.

If this is freedom, then man is indeed bound. He contains only a tiny fraction of all that he needs to be himself. Take away his clothes, his tools, his home, his city, his country, and what is left of him? Take away his crops, and earth and air and water and sunshine, and space that holds them all, and see what remains. Take away his language, and the immense web of social relationships which determine his entire personality, and he is a mere animal—and scarcely that. And even if the more obvious social pressures are somewhat relaxed, and he is left to behave more or less as he likes, what he likes is only what his total past likes: all history moulds his present actions, and true spontaneity is out of the question. He really isn't responsible for his behaviour. Therefore to condemn him is uncharitable and unrealistic, and to insist on reforming him is impertinent. To know all would be to forgive all, because in the end it is the All which is responsible. Any limitation destroys freedom. Not even the most godlike of finite creatures can be blamed for his shortcomings.

In other words, everything short of the Whole is too small to be free. Only the Whole is self-contained, subject to no outside influences, complete, and alone. And anyone who claims to be free is really claiming to be the Whole.

Now it is a fact that I *feel* free, and never question the feeling. What's more, I can make no sense of what I do unless I *am* free. Whenever I deliberately choose this and not that, whenever with full awareness I accept responsibility for what I have done, I am unconditionally asserting the fact that I am free now, and always have been free. How could I take any blame or any praise for actions which are even slightly predetermined? I declare that I am no tool, and am doing what *I* want to do, and all the seemingly overwhelming evidence to the contrary makes no difference at all.

There is only one explanation of these astonishing facts: it is the still more astonishing fact that I *include* everything by which I am conditioned. That is to say, I am free because I am the only one who can be free—the Whole, the Totality, God Himself—and not a man at all. And directly I see this obvious truth and realise just Who I am, I know I have come Home, to Liberty's only source. Now I walk alone, in the sure knowledge that everything is Myself and as I want it. Now I am gay and carefree.

* * * * *

Chapter 40

Aloneness

Man Is In Company: I Am Alone

One man is a contradiction in terms. Even when Douglas Harding is marooned on a desert island, he is never alone. He thinks of men, does things for them, compares himself with them, is continually influenced by then. In a manner of speaking, a man *is* other men.

God, on the other hand, is always alone. God plus man, God plus anything at all, is an absurdity. There is none beside Him.

When I am truly alone, I am He. What is it like, how does it feel, to be this solitary One, absolutely on My own? It is to feel superbly relieved, unconcerned, lightsome. It is to know the thrill and the relaxation of having nobody to please, to fear, to refer to. It is to have won through, to be victorious over the world, and at peace at last. It is to have finally settled accounts with death and all evil, to have nothing to lose or to gain, and to desire nothing whatever. It is to hold no very high opinion of Oneself, and no very low opinion, and indeed no opinion at all, seeing that no standards apply to Me who am incomparable.

Being thus entirely on One's own, quite alone, without a soul to confide in or bear One company, suggests an experience that is either very dull or else very terrifying — since it could hardly be both at once. In fact, it is the reverse of both. *Only* when I am alone am I incapable of boredom: I love My own company: every moment of it is a delight. And it is only when there remains not a particle outside Myself that all possibility of terror is gone: a single outsider, one little thing lost to Me, a refugee from Myself, and I am threatened — or rather, I am lost. It is only when I am absolutely all things and no differences remain that I am Myself and safe Home.

I know that this is the end of the journey, the ultimate haven, because it is impossible to imagine any safer anchorage or any profounder calm. Here is the land of heart's desire, *ultima Thule*, the limit unlimited. Here is the only happy issue, true satisfaction, the best. All growth, all striving, all wanting, is aimed at this: and to fall short of it is always pain. One cannot bear not to be all things and everywhere and always: all alienation is self-alienation, all separation is separation from Oneself. It is misery to be only this man and not that man, only this universe and not that; it is misery to be parted from anything at all. To be finite is suffering; to be in company is suffering; to be one of two is suffering. And to be Alone is the end of suffering, and the only joy which is quite unmixed with sorrow.

* * * * *

Chapter 41

Paradox

Man Abhors Paradox: I Revel In It

Either it is so, or else it isn't: it can't be both at once. It can't be a spade *and* a shovel, black *and* white, true *and* untrue, good *and* evil, Douglas Harding *and* everything but Douglas Harding. That is the way the human mind works. And if it didn't, there could be no law-courts, trade, learning, discussion, or indeed any civilisation at all. Fortunately, man has no use for paradox. He inhabits a common-sense region where it doesn't belong, where opposites remain opposed, and extremes never meet.

They meet here, in My region, where only paradox works, and nothing is itself apart from its opposite. Here are five examples:—

My knowledge is ignorance. It is a fact that in a transparently clear, alert, open, empty mind everything falls exactly into place without any friction or overlapping or left-overs, and here it shines brightly as itself. But if any memories, opinions, expectations, or mental habits (no matter how excellent) are brought to bear upon the object, they upset it and get in the way of true knowledge of it.

My love is indifference. I notice that when I love someone without any reservations whatever I want nothing of him—not his improvement, not his presence, not his love returned, not even his good fortune.

My wealth is poverty. If I divide the universe into two worlds—this small world which I own, and that great one which I don't own—then I am very badly off indeed. Instead, I disclaim both, because I see that in fact I have nothing and am nothing; and that this Nothing is My Hold-all, My inexhaustible Purse.

My power is weakness. If I try to put and to keep this small world in order it is always being thrown into disorder by the world outside. But if I see My total impotence, even in those nearer regions where I might seem to exercise some control, and just let things happen, then a miracle happens too: I see that in fact everything is going on as I want it, and is nothing else than the outflowing of My infinite power.

My existence is non-existence. I see that others are, and I alone am not. Yet it is precisely because of this that I alone really am, and they exist only in Me.

If further instances of paradox are required, this book is full of them. And I am the wildest of them all. I am also the final Reconciliation of all the opposites and the Resolution of all life's contradictions. I have My cake *and* eat it—*and* there's neither cake nor Eater!

* * * * *

Chapter 42

Self-Concern

Man's Business Is Man: Mine Is God

Self-interest is the law: it is minding one's own business that makes the world go round. As God is God's concern, so man is man's; and if it were not so, God wouldn't be God and man wouldn't be man. The proper study of man is himself and his own perpetuation in the world, and God help him if he neglects it. As a matter of fact, God *won't* help him: He's attending to Himself!

Man's success in this self-study requires that he shall see himself as objectively as possible, according himself no divine or privileged status, and reserving for himself no sacred, inviolable enclosure into which the profane scientist is forbidden to pry. Thus he rightly sees himself as a close relation of the higher apes, hardly distinguishable from them in his anatomy; and he may even admit (if pressed) that in his own individual lifetime he has been the inferior of the lowest mammal, the lowest reptile, the lowest fish, the lowest worm. And he may (again, if pressed) see his manhood as no individual achievement, but an entering into the immense heritage that awaits him. Certainly it is his business, it is in his interest, to take possession of this richly humanised world that lies about him, and there is nothing unique at the centre of it which should divert his attention. He is a man among men, and his business is with them.

All this is nothing whatever to do with Me. My business is with God. And since there is only one of Me, since I am unique, My business is Myself, the enjoyment of what I am. Nothing else interests Me. Here I am stationed, at the true Centre of the universe, its Beginning and End, its Origin and its Winding-up, in solitary state: how, then, could I overlook Myself and seek other entertainment? How could I contain — or rather, *be* — the Secret of all things and of Being itself, and interest Myself in anything but that Secret? Actually to *be* this Fountain-head, this sole Source, this unspeakable Power, and yet think nothing of it, or to think about something else, is itself unthinkable. For Me, there is no news but Myself, but that news, always up-to-the-minute, is utterly fascinating and never stale.

Douglas Harding is evidently just a man: careful inspection of him reveals nothing special, and to claim divinity for him would be so ridiculous, so contrary to the observed facts, that it couldn't be taken seriously for a moment. But, just as evidently, I am no man but God Himself, gloriously and wonderfully Alone. I adore Myself. I find Myself enchanting, superb, lovely beyond telling. I *enjoy* being God, and who is there to deny Me that supreme delight?

* * * * *

Chapter 43

Omniscience

Man Knows Little: I Know Nothing — And All

Hindu literature credits the yogi with the ability to make himself as small as an atom, as vast as the universe, as light as air; he can reach out to get what he wants, and control Nature and himself. Now in the course of this enquiry I've found that, while it's obvious no man can claim such powers, I exercise them continually, and so easily I hadn't noticed. As soon as I pay attention to what I see only here, and to what I see going on around Me alone, I realise Who I am and what astounding things I'm capable of. I'm Supernature itself.

Omniscience doesn't figure in the traditional eight yogic powers. And, oddly enough for one so gifted, I certainly am an ignoramus. Of the immense array of facts (most of them unspeakably dreary) about objects ranging from the remotest stars to the particles of this hand, with all their tangled histories, I'm almost totally — and altogether blissfully — ignorant. If I'm God, He's an incurable Dunce: the universe consists of the things He doesn't wish to know. The truth is that omniscience as commonly understood would only be fussing and pettiness multiplied to infinity, and quite absurd. I do indeed know All, and know it in the only possible way — to perfection — but I'm not concerned with anything which, because it's less than All, can never be thoroughly known. The details of the universe arise from hasty and narrow vision: they're the product of insufficient enquiry. For the whole truth about anything is the Whole, namely Myself. Every piece of information is misinformation about Me, who am the only Full Information, the Whole Story, the Truth of the matter. Particular bits of knowledge, therefore, I leave to particular bits of Me (such as Douglas Harding), and the more particular they are the more they are ignorance and not knowledge at all.

I see Myself to be without any parts or complications whatever, as a simple Void; nevertheless I notice that this Self-seeing in no way interferes with the simultaneous seeing of a succession of finite objects. Quite the contrary: it's because they're not really observed at all, except by the way and as the mere filling of this Void, that they're seen as never before, in all their individual glory and unique freshness. In fact, the only way to see anything clearly is to treat it like a very faint star that disappears when directly inspected, and glimpse it through the corner of an Eye that's gazing steadfastly at Nothing.

* * * * *

Chapter 44

Omnipotence

My Power Is Infinite, His Nil

If I'm the omnipotent God, how is it I can't will that chair opposite to move over one inch to the left, or that fly on the window to drop dead, or that cloud to melt into the sky? I try again, harder — and still nothing happens! Even this human body — let alone the universe — refuses to obey my orders, and takes its own time recovering from a common cold.

Well, what is an all-powerful God? One Who promotes, designs, makes, operates, and supervises the universe in all its unimaginable intricacy? If so, I'm certainly not Him. But really there's not a scrap of evidence for any such monster as this works-manager God.

What there is evidence for — conclusive evidence right here — is quite another sort of Divinity: not the manager but the whole Works, this ever-present, clearly visible Void which is the only primary producer, this wonderful Factory of nonexistence endlessly turning out all that exists, this central Generator which, supplying all the world's power, itself runs on no fuel whatever, on sheer Nothingness. Fed from this sole Source, Douglas Harding is powerless to add to or subtract from its energies in the slightest degree, or to divert them by a hair's-breadth from their pre-ordained course. No wonder he can't by wishing shift that chair. Even if he were to push it over with his foot, the action would really be Another's.

In fact, it would be Mine, a function of the infinite power streaming continually from This which I am. And why should

I want to work petty miracles on chairs and flies and clouds, when the whole Creation is My non-stop Miracle, and all of it just as I like it to be? I have only to look at the world to see what it is I require; and if I find fault or want to meddle with anything, it's not I but Douglas Harding who feels like that. He resists the nature of things, seeks some control over it, and is powerless; I concur with it, seek no control over it, and am absolute power. This Factory authorises all its products, but doesn't expect them to approve each other.

Is this sour grapes? Am I only making the best of a bad job of a world, pretending to like what I'm powerless to mend?

Try being God, and see if the whole Creation isn't very good! Finding defects is losing their Origin, undoing the Whole. As in the cobra his poison isn't poisonous, or his faeces dirty, or his metabolism involved, so in Me the universe's troubles aren't at all troublesome. All that My creative power complicates, My absorbing power uncomplicates, reducing it to Simple Perfection. Creator and Saviour, I both make and overcome the world, now.

* * * * *

Chapter 45

Omnipresence

He Stays Man-size, I'm Infinitely Elastic

All the way from tiny man to the infinite God — if only it weren't such an impossible jump, if only it could be negotiated in a few comparatively easy hops! Douglas Harding is plainly man-shaped and man-sized: which means he has reduced that much of the universe to himself, attaching to its volume — a cubic foot or two — the label HERE, while all the rest is THERE. The omnipresent God, on the other hand, reduces the whole universe to Himself, labelling all of it HERE. He's everyone and everywhere, Douglas Harding almost nobody and almost nowhere.

So much for God and man; where do *I* stand? When I say "Come here" what do I mean? I may mean: come to this point, this ink-dot I'm now making on this paper, or come to my right hand, or come to where this body is, or come to this room or house or town of mine, or come to this country or continent or planet or solar system or indeed to this universe of mine — come *here* from over there, to *this* region from that, to *my* place from yours. My own HERE and THIS and MINE, then, clearly range from practically nothing to practically everything under the sun, and beyond it.

Nor is this elasticity a useful fiction or accident of grammar. I speak as I feel. Automatically my "I" swells or shrinks to the measure of each occasion. Thus I don't sit on the seat of my pants which are draped on a chair which is screwed to the floor of a plane which flies: quite simply, *I fly*, all the fifty tons of me. I don't grasp a gun which fires a bullet which kills a man: I — gun and all — kill him, and the law agrees. I don't command a division which uses arms which lose a battle: I lose, and take the consequences. I don't employ a neutron to smash an atom-nucleus: I smash it. That's how I talk and that's how I feel. I'm as much or as little of the universe as I need for doing what I have to do.

Nor is this magnificent (but how unsuspected!) elasticity only a matter of feeling: its practical consequences are immense. It makes a difference if I identify myself with something smaller than a man, such as one of his organs to the detriment of the others. It makes a lot of difference if I identify myself with something bigger than a man, and am happy to kill and be killed for the sake of family or country or race, or even (in the event of interplanetary war) of Earth herself. And it makes the world of difference if I take on responsibility for the entire Cosmos, caring for and loving every creature without exception or preference, totally, till all are embraced in Me, lost and saved in this Omnipresent One.

Besides, this expansion from man to the All, with its other aspect of contraction from man to Nothing, is the honest, objective truth about man, who as mere man and at his own level is a mirage that will stand neither close nor distant inspection. For Douglas Harding (as seen by the receding observer) is not himself without his not-self — without his extended physique, comprising his clothes, tools, house, city, country, planet, sun, galaxy: cut off from this universe-body, which is the only true and living whole of him, he's not human, not alive, not even existent. And again (as seen by the approaching observer) he's resolved into a community of organs, each of which is 'really' a community of cells, each of which is 'really' a community of molecules, and so on down to the featureless substratum, to the central immateriality or Void which he *really* is. So in fact he turns out to be the All-Nothing, the One who is both totally absent from the world and totally present in it; and all the steps — all the degrees of embodiment and disembodiment — on the way to that double goal are just as illusory as he is.

It's the first step which counts. Once I start consciously incorporating anything beyond man — starting with this jacket (a sloughable skin) and this pen (an easily grown and amputated sixth finger) — there's no halting my growth till I incorporate Everything. And once I start looking into what I'm made of, there's no halting my ungrowth till I incorporate Nothing. Once I admit I'm what I look like from *every* range, and what I feel like, and feel for, and take on, I must in the end come to Self-recognition.

In place of this human body is a treasure-house. Having cracked this safe (called Form) and got at its priceless jewel (called the Void), I hold the key to every safe in the world: now every Form is Void. Being this small (but wholly reliable) sample of the world, knowing its inside story, I know, and indeed am, the Whole Story. Being the clarification, the voiding, in fact the enlightenment of every one of the myriad inhabitants of this little human body, I can — I must — go on to become the Enlightenment of all my greater bodies and their inhabitants, including the whole Earth, the stars, the Cosmos itself. All this opaque, vast, inert, dreadfully complicated world is instantly de-Formed, Oned, Enlightened through and through, in My shadowless Omnipresence.

* * * * *

Chapter 46

Discrimination

I Divide God From Man: He Confuses Them

The brightest light casts the deepest shadow, and there is a dark side to the true mystical illumination. This Light is a sudden dawn which turns our night into brilliant Sunshine — and still deeper night. Its colour-scheme is sharp black and white, with no greys whatever, no twilight.

Here, the infinitely searching Daylight of God: there, the human obscurity in which all outlines are blurred. It is the essence of the dark that it can't see how dark it is. Man is man because he fails to realise how narrow and strict his limitations are: if he did he would no longer be human. For to be man is to be in a muddle: it is vastly to overrate the human and underrate the Divine, to think altogether too much of himself and altogether too little of Himself, to fail in every way to distinguish that world from This, so making the worst of both. Paradoxically, while I imagine that — as man — I have a little freedom or originality or power or spirit or divinity, or any other real virtue, I lack them all and am in fact nothing; but directly I take this truth to heart, I am the Nothing whose other aspect is the All that contains every virtue to perfection. I am the unkindly Light that shows up Douglas Harding's total darkness. The razor-keen Sword of Discrimination does indeed sort things out, cutting clean through every strand of connecting tissue between him there and Myself here. In one merciless blow it deals absolute death to him and absolute Life to Me, leaving no half-life anywhere.

Unlike the bogus sort, real piety is severely precise, the enemy of all woolliness and amiable compromise. The fact that, ultimately, even the Sword of Discrimination is sheathed (God and man, Myself and him, Light and darkness, all merging in the undifferentiated Essence) does nothing to blunt its edge meanwhile. On the contrary, premature unification makes the final Unity impossible. Our comfortable moods of being in tune with the Infinite, vague but warm-hearted moments when we're at one with God and Nature and man — these are fine, but before they can issue in the real Union they have to go the way of division and death. The One-beyond-oneness in which the many disappear is no mixture of them and Itself. Any hybrid of the flesh there and the Spirit here is an impossible monster and abortion. The Nameless in which they are for ever reconciled holds them for ever apart.

* * * * *

Chapter 47

Enlightenment

I Am Enlightened, He Is Not

So I really think I'm Enlightened, do I? — Liberated or Awakened or Realised or Enlightened, that is to say, in the sense that Gautama the Buddha was Enlightened under the Bo Tree. This is a big claim. What is the honest truth?

Once more, outside and secondhand information is useless here. It's no good relying on hearsay — on books however sacred, on teachers however revered, on friends however perceptive and frank. Even first-hand inspection, once it has passed over into memory, will not answer this crucial question. Only an immediate test, applied here and now, will settle it beyond any doubt. There's nothing for it but to look and see.

One glance at Douglas Harding, and the very idea of his Enlightenment is ridiculous. It isn't that he hasn't put in enough years of spiritual practice yet, or achieved any kind of holiness of perfection whatever. His trouble is at once much deeper and more obvious. If Enlightenment means anything at all, it means non-duality, and he is many things among many more things; it means clarity, and he is quite opaque; it means changelessness, and he alters from moment to moment; it means simplicity, and he is very complex; it means freedom from the body-illusion, and he is very much a body; it means infinity, and his boundaries are there to see. And so on. All these disabilities are incurable, and the least of them debars him permanently from Enlightenment. The fact is he's not merely incapable of Enlightenment: he's its antithesis, the complete exemplar of all it is not.

This is because he has the bad luck always to turn up in the wrong place at the wrong time. For finding Enlightenment is like finding anything else: one has only to know where it is and when it is there, and then be sure to keep one's appointment with it. *This is an appointment I couldn't miss if I tried.* Enlightenment belongs nowhere but HERE and at no time but NOW. I see, beyond all doubting, at this very moment and on this very spot, this non-dual, lucid, changeless, simple Void which is Myself, and in every way the opposite of the man over there.

And since there can be no such entity as an Enlightened man there, or an Unenlightened Godhead here, it's really nonsense to talk about Enlightenment happening to anyone. It can't be worked up to, earned, achieved. It has never occurred and will never occur. It just is. There's no escaping it.

* * * * *

Chapter 48

Deification

I Know I Am God, He Thinks He Is Man

Is it perhaps possible to see quite clearly Who I am, yet without total identification? When I say 'I', what do I mean? If someone were suddenly to shout 'Douglas Harding!' would I start up less smartly than if he had shouted 'Oh God!'? In short, while no doubt I *understand* I'm God, do I really mean it?

The answer is an unqualified, resounding YES. This seeing is clinched by the profoundest conviction, by a sure and settled inner necessity. I refuse absolutely to be put off with anything less than total identity with God, with the Godhead, the Ultimate Essence Itself. I'm not interested in being loved or saved by Him, or being like Him, or being His Son and co-ruler, or even being united with Him for ever. To be saved is to *be* Him. The alternative is perdition — not so much because it preserves indefinitely some remnant of Douglas Harding (which is intolerable) or divides the One (which is impossible) as because I experience no end to anxiety, no final peace or perfect joy, till I am consciously the All and the Alone. I have no other meaning, no other destiny or need, no other interest whatever, than simply to be Him, which is to say Myself. In other words, because He alone is Rest, I cannot rest *in* Him, but only *as* Him. The slightest haircrack of separation would be as unbearable as — fortunately — it is unnatural and indeed mythical. The truth is that My Godhood, once clearly seen and deeply felt, is so obvious and so certain that it shows up my manhood as a case of mistaken identity, or at least as a temporary convention or artifice, maintained with some difficulty. In a sense, it's far easier to be God than man. It's only a matter of ceasing to pretend.

One is what one wants to be, what one insists on being. My ambition, being infinite, is infinitely satisfied; man's, being moderate and vacillating, is only partially satisfied. Very partially — because in fact the human condition has a basic flaw: it's the product of ignorance: if a man saw what he really was he would see Me, the Whole of him. God is naturally God; men is conventionally man. In the last resort he's a rather arbitrary selection from the facts, from the Totality which is Me. No wonder Douglas Harding can never whole-heartedly believe in himself, or answer to that name quite unhesitatingly. He always has the vague, puzzled, uneasy feeling of not altogether being himself. He isn't. He's Me.

* * * * *

Chapter 49

Spiritual Exercises

He Finds They Work, I Find They Don't

Some masters say that spiritual exercises — and particularly meditation systematically practised, maybe for a lifetime — are indispensable to Enlightenment. Some seem to think them unnecessary. Some go so far as to suggest they're what's standing in our Light. And — to complete our confusion — some say one thing one day and the opposite another day.

This serious practical problem will, like all others, solve itself when we settle whose problem it is. *Who*, if anyone, needs to undergo this arduous spiritual training?

The answer is: all whose Enlightenment isn't yet complete. There have lived a few highly gifted ones whose training was comparatively brief and easy, but for most aspirants it's a very long and hard endeavour, not so much to gain some initial illumination, as afterwards to mature it to the limit. A man gets what he goes in for, which means what he works for methodically, perseveringly, whole-heartedly; and the spiritual life is no exception to this rule. It's useless his sitting back and expecting Enlightenment to drop into his lap: he must climb a very tall and thorny tree and pluck it for himself. The reason he isn't Enlightened is that he doesn't sufficiently want to be, and therefore can't bring himself to make the necessary effort.

No doubt the right sort of spiritual training makes sense and really works for all who seriously try it — *with one exception. I* find it makes no sense whatever and can't possibly work! Consider what it would mean. It would mean I'm anxious to get something, whereas in fact I'm complete. It would mean I'm looking for future results, whereas in fact the Goal is now or never. It would mean drawing comparisons with others' attainments, whereas in fact I'm incomparable. It would mean making enormous efforts to curb the wandering mind, whereas in fact it's trying so hard that's the trouble. It would mean sitting at the feet of some guru, or studying the scriptures carefully, whereas in fact it's this sort of indoctrination which prevents discovery. It would mean dwelling on prescribed ideas (such as impermanence, no-self, non-duality), whereas in fact what's needed is to drop all ideas and stay perfectly open. It would mean cultivating feelings (such as compassion, love, calm) whereas in fact they would only cloud this Emptiness here, this perfect Dispassion. It would mean the hard grind of keeping up one's exercises, so many hours a day, day in and day out for years, in the teeth of all natural impulses, whereas in fact the divine ease and joy I'm seeking so painfully are available here this very instant.

So far as I'm concerned, then, there's something wildly wrong about the very notion of spiritual training. It isn't merely that this training doesn't make for Enlightenment: it rushes off in the opposite direction! A more effective antidote couldn't be imagined! No wonder I've found the everyday, unregenerate human condition much more promising spiritually — or much less unpromising — than this direct path from the Enlightenment here into outer darkness.

Actually — apart from a brief lapse or two — I've never gone in for any spiritual training. I just couldn't work for some remote benefit: the pay-off had to be in sight, or I wasn't interested. Luckily, I happened to be incurably inquisitive as to Who or What I was, and if every moment didn't bring some glimpse of an answer, at least it held an increasing sense of wonder and mystery: the sheer adventure of this search, its unflagging thrill and surprises, needed no other reward. Days, months, years slid by almost imperceptibly. Nor was it a case of enthusiasm living on hope of still better things: whatever I'd just discovered, whatever I saw clearly at the moment — *that* was the whole astonishing truth, in every sense the last word on the subject! How conceited, how absurdly cocksure I was! But never tired, never for one unworthy instant tempted to give up, or even take a holiday.

Looking back, of course, it's possible to adopt a more sober and modest view. Seen in perspective, one's early insights must appear shallow, one's concentration fitful, one's knowledge negligible, one's love undeveloped and choosy, one's behaviour often deplorable. But at the time these defects were ignored in the heat of the pursuit. *Therefore* they tended to go; *therefore* a steady deepening of the whole spiritual life actually occurred. This no-training turned out to be the real training.

But no such backward look has anything to do with Reality, with Me. Because spiritual exercises work in time, they can never work towards This which is out of time. So the final answer to our question *Who has to train?* is: he must, I can't, and let each mind his own business. Here, as in every other respect, we're poles apart: his white is My black, his food My poison, his time-ridden and busy reality My dream — and ultimately not even that. I live in the present — I *am* the Living Present — and all else is imagination and death. ONLY GOD MAKES SENSE.

* * * * *

Chapter 50

Stopping Thought

He's Thinking, I'm Not

Man is the thinking animal. It's his distinguishing feature, his peculiar glory, to form concepts. His early years are devoted to their elaboration, his maturity to their employment, his old age to hanging onto them till the last moment. So we're expected to feel an amused pity, not free from contempt, for the village ancient who replied, when asked how he filled in his time: "Sometimes I sits and thinks, sometimes I just sits." Yet if a Zen monk had said something like that, instead of our pity our respectful congratulations would have been called for, seeing that his whole life is devoted to the immensely difficult task of suppressing thought. For the Masters regard conceptual thinking, even all thinking, as the root of our troubles, and its ceasing as our salvation. The worst of it is, the harder we try to stop thoughts the faster they seem to come — naturally so, because where there's desire there's thinking, specially when the desire is to stop thinking! On the other hand, just to relax and let our minds rip doesn't help either: they give us no peace at all. What in heaven's name, then, *are* we to do?

But first, what are the facts? What and where is this thinking which one authority says is my special privilege and another says is my curse? Is it really mine, or anything to do with me? I have to look into this for myself: obviously I can't leave it to them.

Well, thinking is certainly going on around here. In fact,

the whole world, not excluding that section of it called Douglas Harding, is propped up and held together by thought alone: its supporting framework, without which it would instantly collapse, is that huge interlocking structure of percepts and concepts which from the start I've been erecting around this Spot. Not only all I see and hear, and taste and smell and touch, but also all I imagine or desire or most intimately feel — in short, all things and qualities experienced — are nothing else than this great enveloping thought-structure, suitably coloured and ornamented. When its beams and stancheons start coming apart and falling about me, there goes my aim in life, my reason, and in the end my humanity itself.

What remains? Who is the builder, the mysterious owner-occupier of this vast thought-world, the thinking nucleus around which it has all been constructed — only to fall down one day? Precisely because he's not out there where his thought is elaborated, but right here where it originates, he cannot himself be thought, conceived, described, understood. He can only be seen — clearly seen. I see Myself with unique brilliance and vividness because this seeing — and this alone — is simple sight, unclouded by the slightest mist of thought: by comparison, everything else is glimpsed through a dense conceptual fog. Immediately I stop looking and start thinking about Myself I leave My place and so lose Myself; instead, it's Douglas Harding out there who's being thought of. Literally, I'm *without* thoughts: better, they're *without* Me, going on outside. A man tells Me he's thinking: and so he is. How unlike Me! All is thought where he is, nothing is thought where I am.

However violently the hurricane of discursive thinking sweeps round and round, I'm always its still and thought-free

Eye. Instead of trying — ridiculous idea! — to calm the tempest, I just stay indoors where the gentlest breeze can never creep. So in fact there exists no problem of whether I should put an end to thought, and, if so, how to do it. All that's needed is to distinguish sharply between Myself here, Who am incapable of a single notion, and Douglas Harding there, who's nothing but a bundle of them. So long as we're not muddled up, there's nothing wrong with either of us and nothing to be done.

I lack nothing. Consciously to *be* the mindless Source of all thoughts here, is to *have* the right ones out there — those which fit the occasion because they're allowed to go their own way, as not My concern at all. Because there's no connection between Me and My thought-up universe, no interference, complete detachment, it's all right; any meddling with its thinking processes — let alone their suppression — would make it all wrong. Only let Me attend to Myself here, and so far from thoughts there proving troublesome, they're what make the world go round.

How can this Axle drive the Wheel of Life without itself moving? How is My power transmitted to My world if between Me and it there is no continuity? The real Hub, of course, is not the shaft but its Centre, this dimensionless still point which alone enables the great Wheel to turn, this absolutely powerless central Gap or Discontinuity which is the only real generator of power. In other words, it's because I'm for ever this perfectly thought-free Void that My world, with its infinite riches, is from here so splendidly felt and perceived and conceived into existence out there. It is all indispensable — including Douglas Harding, and his most discursive thinking, and indeed this chapter itself — in spite of the fact, or rather *because* of the fact that it stands in utter contrast to Me.

My entirely thinkable universe, and My entirely unthinkable Self, are in the end inseparable, a simple Unity.

* * * * *

Chapter 51

Self-Confidence

I Alone Have The Courage Of His Convictions.

I have looked here and seen that I am God, and not man. But is this seeing believing? Do I know, through and through, that I am Him? It would hardly be enough to go by what I clearly see, if it gave the lie to what I deeply feel. If one's Godhood had to be tugged and manoeuvred into position and kept there by constant vigilance, instead of riding in smoothly and naturally under its own steam and flying the ensign of utter, utter conviction, it would still be only a wonderful idea. Any lurking doubt whether I am Him would show that I'm not.

Once I go into the matter thoroughly, wholeheartedly, I find I can doubt everything but this supreme certainty, this Conviction which makes all other convictions seem mere notions, this bed-rock Certainty that remains unshaken when every opinion is shattered. I am Him: He is Me. Truly, this is all I know. Everything else was fantasy.

No, it's not God but man who's difficult to believe in. He's the one who has to be contrived, practised, maintained at enormous cost in will-power and vigilance — and then at best with only partial success. Unable to endure the strain of pretending to be what he isn't, he tends always to fall back on what he is, his true Nature. For every man is sure he is God, only he lacks the courage of his convictions: it's his fear of public opinion which in fact constitutes his manhood. A man is a man because he just dare not take himself seriously. Therefore he fights, he labours, he lays plans with astonishing patience and ingenuity, in order somehow to ward off Self knowledge. It is indeed hard to be human, so easy to be God.

Man has only to relax now, as one day he will relax in death, and cease caring what people think, to find that the story of his manhood is pure fiction, an outward pretence it pays to keep up for the sake of a little (but how little!) peace and quiet, while his true inner attitude, and even much of his behaviour, shows he doesn't believe a word of it. His trouble isn't that he doesn't know very well Who he is, but that he daren't admit — even to himself — that he knows; and this timidity is fatal. He defers: he's how he strikes others. I never defer: I'm how I strike Myself. I *am* Self-confidence. And I *dare* him to be himself — which is to be Me.

These are empty words till they are tested in everyday experience. Dropping all expectation and pretence, all attempts to be good or modest or respectable, what do I genuinely feel in the concrete details of everyday living? The startling discovery I make is that *I have always felt the exact opposite of what Douglas Harding was supposed to feel.*

My divinity is no new thing. I started off bursting with Self-confidence. As a very young child I had the feeling (not expressed in words, of course, but more forcibly in actions) that I was the unique, bodiless Centre of the world — of Heaven itself — perfect and beyond criticism, the rightful owner of all things, omnipotent, free, immortal. Growing up consisted in being talked and laughed and spanked out of all this nonsense — more or less. The hard lesson I was supposed to learn was that I was only human after all, that I was not God but only one of the myriad things He'd made, that the world wasn't Heaven but more like a Hell in which

I was usually in the wrong, and always unsatisfied, weak, pushed around by people and things, and doomed to die. I didn't grow up to manhood: I was dragged down, loudly protesting, from Godhood.

Yet secretly I remained what I was. A bad pupil, I refused to be cut down to man-size. Even my growing use of the word "I" proclaimed that I knew Who "I" was. Everything I ever did was really a protest against all imposed and supposed human limitations, a tacit assertion of divinity. For example, only because I was still the Owner of everything could I be so sure I owned anything, and so determined to get more and more, as if to prove I had no limits. Only because I was still Omniscient, could I be so quick to recognise truth immediately I heard it (being reminded of what, evidently, I knew already) and so anxious to go on learning, as if I *must* know all. Only because I was still absolutely Free and Unconditioned could I be so certain that I was responsible for everything I had done, and by some miracle broken the unbreakable fetters of heredity and environment. Only because I was still Omnipotent could I be so absurdly confident (in the teeth of all the evidence) that I was always changing the iron course of events at will, however slightly. Only because I was still the Fortunate One could I be so sure of luck. Only because I was still the Incomparable One could I remain convinced that I was Central, of infinite value, not at all to be classed with others. Only because I was still the Alone could I be content with this profound isolation from all other beings, always. Only because I was still the Immortal One could I live cheerfully under sentence of death, in this condemned-cell of a world.

And so on... These were no mere tokens of essential Godhood. My whole life was a vivid demonstration that I was never really taken in. All that remained was to have the courage of man's deepest convictions, the nerve to admit the divinity I'd always felt and acted upon.

* * * * *

Epilogue

What I Am

In this book, as in life, I have only one aim—to find out what I am.

To have taken for granted that I am something called Douglas Harding would have been to assume the very point at issue, and make nonsense of the inquiry before it began. From the start, therefore, I ignored as far as possible all I had heard or imagined about myself, and just looked again to see whatever was to be seen, and trusted only that. And the result of this self-inspection is the discovery that I am just about as different from Douglas Harding as I could be. I am the opposite of all I once thought I was. Here is no man, but God Himself—right *here*, in the Place where the scriptures say He is.

This discovery—this seeing—proves itself in day-to-day living: nothing else works. Also it is compelling beyond any ordinary experience: it carries total conviction. I can doubt almost anything I see, but not what I see most clearly of all—this Divine Presence, and this human absence. I see God far, far more plainly here than I see any man there.

What light does this throw on man and his terrifying problems?

Before reforming the world, it is prudent to find out who is the would-be reformer. Can what is observed in that place ever be understood, or even clearly seen, if it is regarded as independent of what is observing in this place? The human situation always looks desperate, until it is consciously viewed from the divine situation, here. Heaven doesn't lie around man; man lies around Heaven; and failure to note this is Hell. It is all a question, not of changing a single thing, but of seeing things in their places—God at the centre here, and man at the circumference there, some feet off. Douglas Harding doesn't confront God: God confronts Douglas Harding—with the question: 'However did I seem to get specially involved with *that*?' Douglas Harding must be kept out of this Paradise, and an angel with a two-edged flaming sword of discrimination posted at the gate to prevent him creeping back.

Once the divine and the human are thoroughly unscrambled, everything is put right, everything makes sense, and there is no end to the discoveries, clarifications and new insights which follow. The foregoing chapters are only a sample of the sort of thing that waits impatiently (hidden only by its obviousness and simplicity) to be noticed.

What is needed is not more practice, or more spiritual or mental discipline, or study, or systematic meditation, or any working up of states, but honesty, courage, faith, and single-mindedness—the honesty to see what there is to see without editing it, the courage to take it seriously, the faith to act upon it, and the single-mindedness just to go on being quietly Oneself. Then there are no more problems.

* * * * *

Alone, free and content

I see what man is out there
and that it agrees with what commonsense says of him
and that it is unsatisfactory.

I see what I am here
and that it agrees with what religion says of God
and that it satisfies.

Looking in and out at once, I see
that whatever man is, God is the opposite
and that I have never been human,

and that man is satisfactory too
now I take him as I find him, where I find him,
remote from the emptiness here,
contained in the fullness that is neither here nor there.

I go by what I see
therefore all is well
and I am alone, free and content.

www.ingramcontent.com/pod-product-compliance
Lightning Source LLC
LaVergne TN
LVHW051645080426
835511LV00016B/2505

"I have known Jennifer Taylor since she started her career in the wedding industry. Because of her business strength and education, she has grown her business to include a team of planners who were fortunate to be trained by her.

Jennifer has an amazing sense of detail and structure in how she works. Because of that knowledge, she has become an industry expert and a public speaker/educator as well.

This book boils things down for the engaged couple into a practical format that guides them step by step in the planning process. I personally feel that nothing beats hiring a wedding planning professional, so the couple and their families can be guests at the wedding and not worry about logistics and the myriad of details.

Having this book as a planning guide and a professional planner at the helm for the wedding--success is sure to be achieved!" --Chérie Ronning, President, Wedding Network USA, LLC

"This should be required reading for not only every couple planning a wedding, but also all wedding vendors who want to serve their clients to the best of their ability. Jennifer includes not only her own priceless personal insight from the planner's perspective, but also what is basically a fantastic beginner course on all the little things you didn't know you needed to be aware of when starting to plan your wedding. I've been in the wedding business for over ten years and learned plenty of things I didn't even know! I wish all of my clients had a copy of this book."
Amy Soper, Amelia Soper Photography

"When I got engaged in 2016, I was absolutely thrilled. It's the moment that every girl dreams about, but then reality sets in and you realize you have to start planning a wedding. Like most brides, I thought to myself, 'Where do I even start?' This book led me in the right direction and didn't completely overwhelm me with information. It took me step by step and told me everything I needed to know, without feeling like I needed to make all of these decisions right away. I would recommend this book to anyone starting to plan their wedding who needs a guide. You can read a few lessons at night and really enjoy the process of planning your wedding. Thank you, Jen, for guiding me in the right direction and teaching me not to sweat the small stuff. It's all about having fun and enjoying the experience. I truly appreciate it!" --Emily Harris, married 2018

"I've said for years that someone needs to hand brides a cheat sheet on navigating wedding confusion, before they even take on a planner, and Jen Taylor has! Six-Word Lessons for a Stress-Free Wedding *is the must have 'where to start' road guide for brides."* –Anne Timss Makeup and Hair